"Informative. Insights [into] why classical music's most analyzed instrument retains so many mysteries."   —*San Diego Union-Tribune*

"Entertaining. . . . [Marchese] shows a talent for engaging turns of phrase, and his accessible style and dry humor commingle well."
—*Library Journal*

"In exploring the relationships to one another of Antonio Stradivari of Cremona, Sam Zygmuntowicz of Brooklyn, Eugene Drucker of Manhattan, and a violin made of spruce and maple, Marchese corrals the acoustics and technology of violin building, the love of violin making, and the history of seventeenth-century Italian violins into one book. Like *The Piano Shop on the Left Bank*, this exploration of the lore of musical instrument manufacture is easy, entertaining, and uniquely informative reading."   —*Booklist*

"A fascinating and engaging story about musicianship as well as the art of the violin maker. This book is a treat."   —*Decatur Daily*

"In our flimflam, fast-food world of convenience, it's exhilarating to learn that the old-timey craft of violin making still exists in Brooklyn. John Marchese, one of our best literary journalists, explores the life of colorful Sam Zygmuntowicz, a retro perfectionist with the delicate artistic fingers of Antonio Stradivari. *The Violin Maker* is a magical, profound, and elegant look at the continued need for high quality in our throwaway society."
—Dr. Douglas Brinkley, professor of history at Rice University
and author of *The Great Deluge*

"Nobly upholding and carrying forth the tradition of John McPhee and Tracy Kidder, John Marchese chronicles the extreme craftsmanship and sharp-edged personality of a world-class craftsman. Between the lines, he wittily deconstructs the capacious lore of violin making, from Stradivari to the twenty-first century. Readable and engaging from the downbeat to the coda."

—Ben Yagoda, author of
About Town: The New Yorker *and the World It Made* and
When You Catch an Adjective, Kill It:
The Parts of Speech, for Better
and/or Worse

the

VIOLIN
_____
MAKER

Also by John Marchese

RENOVATIONS: A FATHER AND SON
REBUILD A HOUSE AND
REDISCOVER EACH OTHER

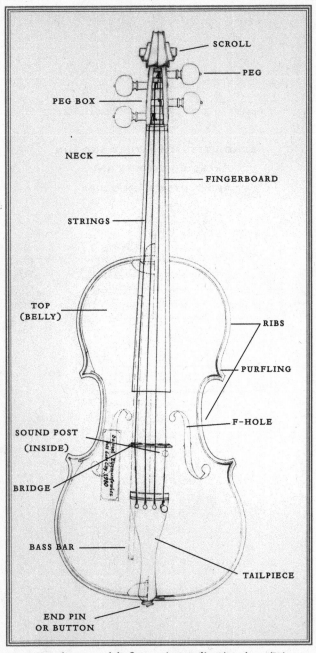

SCROLL

PEG

PEG BOX

NECK

FINGERBOARD

STRINGS

TOP
(BELLY)

RIBS

PURFLING

F-HOLE

SOUND POST
(INSIDE)

BRIDGE

BASS BAR

TAILPIECE

END PIN
OR BUTTON

Based on a model of Antonio Stradivari's, circa 1715.
Drawing by Sam Zygmuntowicz.

the
VIOLIN
MAKER

*A Search for the Secrets
of Craftsmanship, Sound,
and Stradivari*

JOHN MARCHESE

HARPER ⬤ PERENNIAL

NEW YORK • LONDON • TORONTO • SYDNEY • NEW DELHI • AUCKLAND

HARPER ● PERENNIAL

FIRST HARPER PERENNIAL EDITION PUBLISHED 2008.

Illustration on page iv by Sam Zygmuntowicz

Designed by Lorie Pagnozzi

The Library of Congress has catalogued the hardcover edition as follows:

Marchese, John.
    The violin maker: finding a centuries-old tradition in a
Brooklyn workshop / John Marchese.—1st ed.
        p. cm.
    Includes bibliographical references (p.).
    ISBN 978-0-06-001267-0
    1. Zygmuntowicz, Sam. 2. Violin makers—New York
(State)—New York. 3. Violin—Construction—New York
(State)—New York. 4. Drucker, Eugene, 1952–5.
Violinists—United States. I. Title.

ML424.Z94M37 2007
787.2'19092—dc22   2006052182
[B]

ISBN 978-0-06-001268-7 (pbk.)

16 17 18 19 20 DR/RRD 10 9 8 7 6 5 4 3

To four people who helped in so many ways
to make it possible for me to write any book, but who
didn't get to see this one:

John Marchese
Rosemary Marchese
Santino Marchese
Phyllis Marchese

Contents

Contents

Acknowledgments

First off, I have to thank Hana Smith for her contributions to this book.

The two men at the center of *The Violin Maker*, Sam Zygmuntowicz and Eugene Drucker, were in many ways collaborators as much as subjects. Sam graciously opened his workshop and spent many, many hours allowing me to look over his shoulder while he worked. I greatly appreciate the time he took to tutor me in the intricacies of his craft and his patience while trying to teach someone whose learning curve is often shaped more like a parabola.

Gene generously gave me opportunities to watch him make music and teach music and openly shared his thoughts and feelings. His musicianship is enlightening and inspiring. His literary skills will soon be on display with the publication of his first novel, *The Savior*.

In some way, both men inform nearly every page, though, of course, any mistakes or inaccuracies are mine alone.

Thanks to the nice folks who worked in the Brooklyn workshop: Wiltrud Fauler, Dietmar Schweizer, and Gladys Thomas Toscano.

My appreciation also to the other members of the great

Emerson String Quartet—Phil Setzer, Larry Dutton, and David Finckel—who were always friendly and helpful, and, along with their colleague, remarkable and inspiring musicians. Da-Hong Seetoo, their brilliant producer and engineer, was great fun to be with.

I owe a debt to the Violin Society of America and the people who run and participate in the annual workshops for violin makers and acousticians at Oberlin College. They are top craftsmen and researchers who are pushing the art of violin making forward in its fifth century. They willingly shared their knowledge, expertise, jokes, food, and booze. They include: Gregg Alf, Pam Anderson, Tom Croen, Joe Curtin, John Dilworth, Chis Dungey, David Folland, Chris Germain, Feng Jiang, Francis Morris, Frank Ravatin, Ben Ruth, Ray Schryer, Fan Tao, Marilyn Wallin, David Wiebe.

At HarperCollins, Marjorie Braman was the person who lit the spark for this book. When the resulting flame seemed like it might become eternal, she showed great patience. And when there was finally a manuscript, she deftly guided it with a sure hand and a light touch. Every writer should be so lucky.

Once again, my agent, David Black, came through in the clutch. If only the Jets would draft him.

Last and most, I have to thank Jana DeHart, my living companion, traveling companion, erstwhile research assistant, and irrepressible scout. She helped in so many ways that to say this book couldn't have been done without her would be a gross understatement.

the

VIOLIN

MAKER

Chapter 1

THE MAGICAL BOX

This story is about a craftsman entering the prime of his career who let me follow him as he tried to build a musical instrument that might top the work of the man who many think is the greatest craftsman who ever lived. His name was Antonio Stradivari, and he died more than 250 years ago.

Not long after I first met Sam Zygmuntowicz in Brooklyn, he invited me to join him in Ohio, where he was spending two weeks that summer teaching at a workshop of violin makers held at Oberlin University. The town of Oberlin is a quiet and neat place that seems to just pop out of cornfields about thirty-five miles southwest of

Cleveland. The college dominates one side of the town with a mix of Gothic and modern buildings set on plush, trimmed lawns. There is a green and shady central square with clumps of tall trees that is dotted with monuments to fallen soldiers and murdered missionaries.

I drove to Oberlin in the first week of July, and the weather was shockingly hot and sticky. The shade of the square would have been a cool refuge at midday were it not for the fact that the college concurrently was hosting a festival of Scottish culture. Each day, bagpipers strolled on the thick grass under the tall trees, blew up their bellows, and emitted that ineffable sound that always makes me think a small farm animal is being slaughtered.

So, like me, most of the violin makers avoided the square at bagpipe time. It seemed a strange coincidence that aficionados of the world's most annoying musical instrument would be in the same small midwestern town as two dozen people obsessed with the world's most glorious musical tool. They didn't mingle. The bagpipe has its fans, of course. Tucked under the right armpit, the windbag can sound less than noxious. I have heard an African-American man in Philadelphia play good jazz on the thing. And on the green and shady lawn of a cemetery, pumping out "Amazing Grace," the bagpipe can sound sublime.

In fact, I had been to a funeral not long before traveling to Oberlin, and that funeral, in a strange way, had helped bring me here. The former governor of Pennsylvania, Robert Casey, had died in his hometown of Scranton, and he was buried after a large and elaborate mass at the city's Catholic cathedral. I was hired to play trumpet in a brass quartet that supplemented the church organ on regal processional music and accompanied a large choir through serious liturgical hymns. The choir loft was packed with instrumentalists and singers added for this special service.

In the midst of the mass, after communion had been taken, a young man who sat near me stood among the gathered musicians and tucked a violin under his chin. He then played, accompanied by only a soft piano, the former governor's favorite song. It was Irving Berlin's "How Deep Is the Ocean." Typical of Berlin, the song makes a lot out of little. The range is barely more than an octave. There are no long leaps between any two notes. The melody climbs through its range in a series of relaxed steps, like an old man on a staircase. It is a simple, pretty tune.

My guess is that the violinist may never have heard the seventy-year-old song before he'd been asked to play it. He was only a teenager, just finishing high school and headed for a top music conservatory—not a prodigy, really, but a talent. That was evident from the first phrase of the song, as he dug his bow into the thick low string of the fiddle. The kid had *a sound*.

The church was packed with politicians, many of whom seemed more interested in being noticed than in mourning their dead colleague. But the moment that kid made his first notes on the fiddle, the crowd stilled and all the extraneous noise seem to rush from the church as from a vacuum. For the next few minutes, as the boy played

Berlin, there was virtually no other sound in the large marbled vault. Even the accompanying piano seemed to disappear.

The violin in its low register sounded like a beautiful moan. On the second time through the chorus, the young man leaped to a higher octave and added more vibrato. The song became a sigh. The voice of the violin was singing without words. He climbed higher for the last notes—in the lyrics a final question: *"How high is the sky?"*—and it made the air in the church seem like crystal, like it could be shattered with a touch. When the violin stopped there was a long, long moment where it seemed the hundreds of listeners held their breath, lest they break the spell.

I have played the trumpet professionally for twenty-five years, never at a high level, but often with very good musicians. If I think of all the music created in the hundreds of gigs I've played, that one tune in a church—a Tin Pan Alley standard interpreted by a teenager with talent—is a highlight. It may have been the special circumstances, yet the more I wondered why, I came to think that it was the sound of the violin. The standard encyclopedia of music, Grove's, explains it simply and authoritatively: "The violin is one of the most perfect instruments acoustically." Acoustic perfection seems like something that can be measured and quantified, and, I would find, many have tried. But the sound of a violin eludes the grasp of mere numbers.

After the mass, on the sidewalk outside the church, I ran into a big city newspaper reporter I know, a tabloid guy who covers politics and who is typically tough and cynical. "When that violin played I nearly lost it," he told me. "I think everybody did."

I didn't say anything then—I might not even quite have known it myself—but after those few minutes listening to the young violinist in the church, my goal would be to find something. I wanted to learn what makes the violin so special. How is it that this hunk of wood with the funny shape can express so perfectly the deepest and most profound human emotions?

I thought of my own musical experience, my life as a listener. As a music student in college, I had to work my way through the standard symphonies. I did a pedagogical survey of jazz and studied most intently the great trumpeters, something I still do. But as the years passed and music became more my avocation—my love, not my living—I was drawn to the sound of strings. Sure, I still might listen to jazz at dinner, or put on a symphony for Sunday morning. But at those times when the lights went out and I really wanted to *listen,* to let sound take me either out of myself or farther in, it was Pablo Casals playing Bach's unaccompanied cello suites, say, or a performance of Beethoven's late string quartets.

I suppose my new search could have begun with violin lessons, but it seemed awfully late in the game for that, and I had enough trouble keeping up with the demands of the instrument I already knew how to play. One of the greatest violinists of all time, Eugene Ysaye, wrote,

"The violin is a poet whose enigmatic nature may only be divined by the elect." Wouldn't that be the people who *build* them?

I did what people do nowadays—typed "violin makers" into an Internet search engine. Immediately, I had a dozen names, but Sam Zygmuntowicz stood out. First, because his surname seemed unpronounceable—it's Zig-mun-toe-vich. Secondly, since he lived and worked in Brooklyn, I could get to his shop by subway from my apartment in lower Manhattan. As I got to know him and the world of violins, I would realize that I'd made a lucky choice. Violin makers, I would learn, can argue a lot about little things, but there would not be much debate that Sam is among the best and most successful violin makers working today. Sure, he told me when I got him on the phone, he wouldn't mind someone watching him make a violin.

And so, a month later, my pilgrimage into the world of fiddles began in earnest with a trip to Oberlin, Ohio.

I arrived a few days after the workshop began. Two dozen violin makers had taken over the college's sculpture studio, a long basement room, with a wall's length of workbenches under a high bank of windows just above ground level. They worked all day and long into the night, with breaks for impromptu symposia on subjects that then seemed hopelessly arcane to me. At one, there was a heated discussion on how to cut perfect miters for the purfling, the thin strips of inlaid wood that run around the edges of a fiddle. At another, a violin maker from Michigan showed everyone how to make casts of famous old instruments using newfangled resins used in automotive design in Detroit. Twelve hours later, people were still making casts. Obviously, this was dedication that bordered on obsession.

Some of the participants in the workshop were officially instructors and some were students, but the division seemed blurry. Around five each afternoon, the classmates started cracking open wine and whiskey bottles, and began a working cocktail hour. Then they moved to a campus dormitory for a communal dinner lubricated with wine and beer. Then back to the studio for more work. By then, nearly everyone was a little blurry. It was late on another hot day in Oberlin that a violin maker from Boston and I sat outside in the chirpy and muggy night, sprawled on a loading dock behind the art studio, hoping to catch a breeze. Inside, his colleagues were still carving away at fiddles well past midnight.

"It's amazing," he told me, "that people like me come here from all over the country and the world, and get together to do what we do for a living. And all we really do for a living is make boxes."

Of course, this made the job seem a lot less interesting and compelling than I imagined. A mere box could not have frozen those hundreds who attended the governor's funeral. Building just a box would hardly attract a few dozen professionals to this torrid little town to spend their summer vacation working at their craft. But before I could question the violin maker he explained it all.

"The thing is," he said, "they're magical boxes."

Chapter 2

THE LUTHIER

The magical box is smaller than a bread box and just about infinitely more complex. There are at least sixty-eight different pieces in a violin, and usually seventy, because finding a large unblemished piece of wood is rare, so the belly and back plates typically are made by joining two pieces. Except for a few metal screws that help make minute adjustments in the tuning of the strings—and the strings themselves—every bit of the thing is made of wood.

This is an object that is formed with a thousand cuts. They start with the roughest—the felling of a tree in the forest—and get progressively smaller and more painstaking. In the late stages of construction, the difference between right and wrong is measured in millimeters, often fractions of that. Building a violin begins in butchery and ends in surgery.

They are called luthiers, the builders. The name is derived from the lute, a bulbous guitarlike instrument that was all the rage in medieval music, and the term is now applied to those who make or repair a whole range of descendants and relatives, from fiddles to guitars. Though its origin is traced back to a primitive stick-like thing called the rebec played by Moorish nomads in the first millennium, the violin as we know it appeared rather suddenly in the middle of the sixteenth century. In little more than a hundred years its design was perfected. The laws that govern the building of this box were decided upon a short time before the laws of gravity were discovered, and they have remained remarkably unchanged since then. It is commonly thought that the violin is the most perfect acoustically of all musical instruments. It is quite uncommon to find someone who can explain exactly why. One physicist who spent decades trying to understand why the violin works so well said that it was the world's most analyzed musical instrument—and the least understood.

Consequently, a luthier, a really good one, is at once a woodworker, an engineer, an historian, a mechanic, and a shaman. What kind of person takes up this trade?

"My parents were Polish concentration camp survivors," says Sam Zygmuntowicz. "They resettled in Sweden and moved to Philadelphia in 1952. I was their first child born in America. My father started a laundry business.

"From a very young age I was highly involved with art. I won a couple of school art contests for sculpture. My older brothers had studied violin but didn't continue, so I wasn't offered violin lessons. I was interested in music though, and I finally took a few guitar lessons when I was around seven years old. Then I picked up the recorder on my own. I got interested in traditional folk music and bought a five-string banjo when I was thirteen and taught myself to play.

"Later that year my family moved, and near our new house was a drainage ditch leading to a park. There were some bamboolike reeds growing there, which I thought would make good flutes. I went to the library and looked for books on flute making. Of course, I didn't find much. I did find a big book on organology, and from that I gleaned some information about Aztec bone flutes and such. I also found a book on guitar making and another that was an introduction to instrument acoustics.

"But the most important book I found was a charming old book called *Violin-Making as it was, and is*. I think that book inspired quite a number of current violin makers."

Sam had sent me this biographical sketch by e-mail before we'd actually met in person. I made a date to visit his studio the next week. Before that, I went to the New York Public Library to see if it had a copy of *Violin-Making as it was, and is*. The book was available, but reading it wasn't easy, because the copy at the library was old and rare. Before I was allowed to touch it the librarians confiscated any pens in my possession and made me wear white gloves. This made note taking too difficult, so I just paged through and read bits. I tried to appreciate how this peculiar book could inspire a young man like Sam Zygmuntowicz, but I have to admit that at first the book's main inspiration on me was a pronounced drowsiness.

If this was the key to understanding the motivation to modern lutherie, it was an odd one. Published in 1885 by a polymath Edwardian dandy named Edward Heron-Allen, this amateur's guide to the world of fiddles is one of the most eccentric books I'd ever seen, full of untranslated phrases in Latin and Greek, poems in tribute to the violin, and a guide to building a fiddle so exhaustive and detailed that you'd have to assume the author suffered from attention surfeit disorder. Later, when I asked Sam what it was about this book that inspired him so much, he said:

"It just made violin making seem romantic."

There was one thing I'd written down after reading Heron-Allen, when the librarians gave me my pens back. His primary injunction as he begins the treatise is this: "Given: A log of wood. Make a violin."

That's the process I wanted to pursue with Sam: watch him take a log and turn it into a fiddle, follow the instrument from its roughest stage to its first performance. If I were a romantic like Mr. Heron-Allen, I might quote Henry Wadsworth Longfellow to describe what I was hoping to see.

Fashioned of maple and of pine,
That in Tyrolean forests vast
Had rocked and wrestled with the blast;
Exquisite was it in design,
Perfect in each minutest part,
A marvel of the lutist's art

But I was heading for Brooklyn and was more than willing to settle for a little less romance.

It was a cool and sunny spring day when I first went to meet Sam. On the subway to Brooklyn, I tried to guess what he would look like. Was there some kind of badge or special outfit that a luthier could wear to give a signal of his status, like the way a white lab coat says *doctor*? Could he, like an auto mechanic, wake in the morning and slip into his trade by donning a stiff set of matching pants and shirt with his name stitched over the shirt pocket?

Apparently not.

My first glimpse of Sam Zygmuntowicz was through a chain-link fence. I was standing on a littered sidewalk on Dean Street in Brooklyn, across the street from the busy loading dock of a tile and flooring store whose front doors faced Flatbush Avenue, a main, wide artery of the borough, where I'd just fought my way across four lanes of angry traffic. Behind us was downtown Brooklyn, a mid-rise cluster of fancy stone structures from a more prosperous past, and a few glassy new buildings that promoters were pointing to as signs of Renaissance for the borough. A few blocks in the other direction was Park Slope, a neighborhood of tree-lined streets and impressive brownstones, one of New York's great gentrified enclaves, set on a rising hill that begins at the famously polluted Gowanus Canal and runs up to Frederick Law Olmsted's Prospect Park. I knew that Zygmuntowicz lived in a row house in Park Slope and that he commuted to work (usually on foot) in this adjacent neighborhood that was still so nondescript and generally bereft of charm that on the day of my first visit the real estate people had still not invented a cute new name for it.

The chain-link fence through which I spotted Sam surrounded a small, unpaved, and weedy driveway leading to the loading dock of a converted six-story factory building, where at one time workmen inside the brick walls and wired windows had manufactured stuff like sporting goods. Now, most of the space is residential and a lot of the residents work where they live, occupied doing new cottage industries like producing video, or art, or, in Sam's case, violins, violas, and cellos. He'd lived in this building for a while, before he got married and started having children.

To say that Sam Zygmuntowicz didn't look like I expected a violin maker to look is absolutely true. But what difference does it make, since I didn't know then what I was expecting? The image didn't come to me until months after this first meeting, when Sam, a little frustrated by the simple-minded questions I was asking him, said testily, "I hope you're not going to do what people have a tendency to do with violin makers: make me seem like a kindly old wood carver—like Geppetto."

Banish the thought, I told him at the time. But when I considered the question later, I realized that the old man who'd carved Pinocchio was kind of what I was hoping for.

That first morning, Sam came across the parking lot to unlock the heavy Master lock on the swinging gate of the fence. He gave a small wave as he emerged from the building and walked slowly toward me. He was, like me, a middle-aged man of average height and medium build, who somehow looked shorter and heavier than he really was. And he was dressed nothing like Geppetto. No suspenders, no heavy leather apron, no knickers. He had a youthful and friendly face, a little mottled, and wore large glasses. His hair was thick and wiry, black with some touches of gray. He was wearing what I would learn is his characteristic outfit: comfortably cut dark cotton chinos and a plaid flannel shirt. On his feet he had leather sandals over dark socks.

The gate between us opened, Sam stuck out his hand and said, "You found it all right?" Then he glanced around for a moment, a little shy and embarrassed by the banality of his question. I was standing in front of him, wasn't I? "Of course you found it all right," he said, and swung the gate open wide to let me through. He locked up behind me and led me across to the building. We trudged up four flights of wide stairs and arrived at a landing with a big steel door. Sam pushed it open, and we entered his studio.

Inside was a scene similar to any number of lofts I'd visited around New York. The exterior walls were concrete and pocked in places. The wood floors showed some scars. Sun poured in through high windows that filled most of the south wall. Just inside the door sat an ebony baby grand piano on a well-worn carpet, a few plants flanking its keyboard, and a music stand tucked into the curve of the soundboard. To the right was a seating area with a broken-in maroon couch and mismatched chairs placed on another threadbare carpet. Every item of furniture seemed to come from the kind of store that some would call *antique* and others *thrift*.

Beyond that there were some homemade cubicles that created a hallway leading to a kitchen where I could glimpse the corner of a giant old commercial stove and table. On a cabinet leading to the hall was a big marionette dressed in a tuxedo, holding a violin in one wired hand and a bow in the other. (This was long before his Geppetto complaint, but Sam would later assure me that he had no hand in carving this fiddle-playing puppet.)

Across from the puppet was a glass-fronted barrister's bookcase, and as we passed it I tried to catch the titles of a few of the books stuffed inside. *Understanding Wood*. *The Violins of Antonio Stradivari*. And, of course, *Violin-Making as it was, and is*.

Although most of the loft had a thrown-together, do-it-yourself feel, this bookcase sat against a new wall that looked professionally built. To the left of it was a pair of polished doors in a buff rosewood finish. Just to the side of those doors hung a small black-and-white framed photo of Sam standing with Isaac Stern, the two of them holding a fiddle together and lifting it toward the camera. On the photo was an inscription from the legendary violinist that read "To Sam, thank you again for your wonderful craftsmanship."

I had read what I could about Sam before coming to visit, and I knew that this was one of the most prestigious commissions of his career, one that had generated a buzz about him in the relatively small and insular world of violins. Maestro Stern was among the faction of top soloists who preferred the fiddles of Giuseppe Guarneri, known in his time around Cremona, Italy, as del Gesù. If the violins of the older and more productive Antonio Stradivari were considered the Rolls-Royce of the trade, those made by Guarneri del Gesù were on the order of Jaguars—more erratically made, but powerful and distinctive. Stern had long played one of the most coveted of Guarneris, called the Panette (most top violins have been labeled at some point in their lifetime, usually by a dealer appropriating some cachet from a famous previous owner). The famous soloist had heard of this young, up-and-coming luthier named Zygmuntowicz who was gaining a reputation for his careful copying of famous instruments. Stern commissioned a copy of the Panette. After it was built, Stern brought the new instrument to a rehearsal with some of his friends, including Yo-Yo Ma, and played it without mentioning that it was a duplicate. Until the great old violinist said something himself nobody noticed he was not playing his regular great old violin. Soon, Maestro Stern asked Sam to copy his other great Guarneri, the Ysaye. Word spread quickly, and Sam's reputation climbed.

"Someday, maybe, I'll tell you the story of that fiddle,"

Sam told me. Then he pushed open those double doors and led me into the workshop of his studio, the inner sanctum of his professional life.

From talking on the telephone with him, I had a basic understanding of how the business worked. Unlike some luthiers, who produced fiddles and then sold them through dealers, Sam took commissions from violinists themselves and then designed each fiddle for the particular player. He was able to make between six and eight violins in a year. (He also usually had one cello in the works at any given time.) When we met his price was $27,000 for a violin and $46,000 for a cello. Because he had more customers than hands, the wait from commission to delivery was about two years, and the larger cello could take five.

"Usually," Sam said, "when I talk to people about violin making I don't get that technical. I talk about the business aspects, the people aspects—things that are understandable to people who have similar concerns in their own field."

I was interested in the business and personal aspects of his trade, of course, but entering Sam's studio for the first time, looking around, I found myself focused on the technical part. The technical part seemed like a wonderful mystery made manifest all around me—a tableau of saws and chisels, files and brushes, stained jars filled with pigments and solvents. Everywhere—on tables, hanging from wires, tucked into storage slots—were the familiar parts of fiddles: the curved, feminine-shaped backs and bellies, the nautilus twist of the scrolls, the flat, dark wedge of the fingerboard.

The workshop had a main room about twenty feet wide and fifteen feet deep, with a windowed wall lined with a workbench that was actually a jerry-rigged progression that began with an old wooden desk on one end and progressed through a series of grafts that included tabletops and built-in counters, supported by legs and drawers. Sam spends most of his workday seated in a padded modern office chair on the left. To his right sat a young woman with thick, light brown hair and an equally thick Austrian accent. Her name is Wiltrud Fauler, and she is one of two assistants that Sam has imported from Europe. The other, Dietmar, soon emerged from a small room in the far right side of the shop, looking like a factory worker in his blue apron smock, except he was barefoot. Both Wiltrud and Deitmar were friendly but had a pronounced shyness and reserve that seemed natural for folks who spend their workdays concentrating on things and not on people. After we were introduced and exchanged a few pleasantries, they quickly turned their attention back to their workbenches and over the next few hours said very little and that, mostly, to each other in German.

Sam Zygmuntowicz didn't miss the irony of a child of Jewish Holocaust survivors hiring two assistants who were German. He was a practical businessman.

"In Germany," Sam told me, "it's quite different from here. They take pride in putting out things of very high quality. It's a very honorable thing. It's a career track much earlier. And it's not like the kids with discipline problems get stuck in the vo-tech school."

Sam had his share of discipline problems while getting through school in Philadelphia. His mother kept many of his report cards, and they were full of complaints about a boy who kept a messy desk and didn't always pay attention. When he began to focus on violin making as his future, his parents couldn't fathom lutherie as an occupation for their son and tried to get him an apprenticeship with the local carpenter's union. At fifteen he landed a job helping to repair school violins at a Philadelphia music store called Zapfs. When he was eighteen he enrolled in the Violin Making School of America in Salt Lake City. It was founded by a German immigrant named Peter Paul Prier, who'd learned the trade in Mittenwald, a Bavarian town with an intense tradesman culture that produced thousands of violins in the last century. The only equivalent to Mittenwald was Mirecourt, a town in France's Vosges mountains, where violin making was an honored and prolific town trade. After college Sam worked for five years in the Manhattan restoration shop of René Morel, a Frenchman who'd trained in the workshops of Mirecourt.

"I guess I consider myself only a demi-American in my work attitude," Sam says. The route that took him from reading Heron-Allen as a teenager in the Philadelphia library to running his own thriving shop in Brooklyn is, he understands, not a journey that most people today want to travel.

"Our society has gotten more materialistic," he says.

"People go into professions to make money. There's nothing like the traditional craft that you do in your village, where you go into it when you're twelve and seven years later your apprenticeship is done and for five years after that you're a journeyman and by the time you're twenty-five you can be a master, and maybe by the time you're thirty you can open your own shop.

"You can't even legally hire a twelve-year-old in this country. It's just not set up that way. And most people who go into violin making don't go into it seeing it simply as an honorable craft—like being a drywall taper or a plumber. People consider it a kind of art, and they go into it with the expectations people bring to art. Or for a lot of people, being a violin maker is kind of like being a boat builder: something slightly romantic, an alternative lifestyle thing.

"Because of that I don't think people get the kind of training that they should get, because that's not what they went into it for. They didn't get into it to get yelled at by a Frenchman in very colorful ways."

The Frenchman he was referring to was his former boss, René Morel, whose craftsmanship is highly respected and whose mercurial nature is widely known. Many of the world's top fiddle players come to Morel to maintain and repair their instruments. And many of the instruments they bring are among the most valuable on earth. In a small gem of a book called *The Countess of Stanlein Restored,* the writer Nicholas Delbanco follows the restoration of a Stradivari cello by that name, which belonged to his father-in-law, the eminent musician Bernard Greenhouse. Greenhouse had waited decades to have his beloved instrument given a major overhaul. And he would trust the job only to Morel.

During his time at Morel's shop on West Fifty-fourth Street in Manhattan, Sam told me, "I used to sit at lunch with a two-million-dollar violin open on my worktable, and just stare at it, trying to understand it, trying to take it in." After he left the employ of Morel and opened his own shop, Sam's reputation grew on his ability to make uncanny copies of old instruments, as he did for Isaac Stern. "If imitation is the sincerest form of flattery," Sam wrote once, "it is also the most direct route to learning a complex and elusive aesthetic."

Sitting with him this first day, listening to him talk, catching glimpses of the work routine of Wiltrud and Dietmar, I began to get a feel for the workaday aesthetic of his shop. It seemed like a wonderful place to spend your time. A high-end sound system supplied a subdued soundtrack. I could see that many of the CD cases stacked near the stereo were classical recordings—a number were by clients he had mentioned—but what came out of the speakers this morning was an eclectic mix of folk and bluegrass and only a little classical. Sam is a self-taught fiddler who plays folk, country, klezmer, swing—everything *but* classical music. Wiltrud is a classically trained violinist who plays with a semiprofessional orchestra in New York. (Dietmar plays just enough to test fiddles in the shop.) "Wiltrud teases me," Sam says, "that I like to listen to hillbilly music."

Surrounding Sam were tools. A series of gougers

looked like elongated woodhandled spoons ranging in size from a few inches to a foot long, their tips ground to a sharp edge to rip through wood. My eye lighted on a set of wood planes. The largest was the same size I have used myself, the kind you buy in a hardware store to get rid of extra wood on doors that don't close right. But in this shop the planes get increasingly smaller, and lined up they look like a set of unnested Russian dolls, shrinking down to a little shoe-shaped thing that is about the right size to jump around a Monopoly game board. To use it, you'd have to hold it between two fingers like the handle of a teacup.

In my library trip before coming to Brooklyn, I'd read some of the articles Sam had written about his craft over the years, mostly for the top journal of the string world, the English magazine called *The Strad*. In one piece, Sam described his work as "more than a complicated carpentry project." But to someone like me, walking into his shop for the first time, it appeared that what he does is *exactly* a complicated carpentry project. Almost everything in the workshop seemed designed to fashion and transform wood. And, leaving out the small room with large band saws that Dietmar worked on sporadically through the morning, everything has a look of timeless tradition. A few tools look so weathered that it seems Stradivari himself could have handled them.

"The fact is," Sam said, "my shop in many ways could be any shop throughout history. Some of the tools are more sophisticated—clamps and things. We have electric lights and we heat glue in an electric pot. But I would say that

Stradivari could walk into this shop and, after a few hours of looking around, could work here quite comfortably."

This was the first of many times that Sam would drop the famous name Stradivari into the conversation. Over the months that followed, I would come to realize that the influence of the Italian craftsman who died in 1737 is felt almost constantly by modern violin makers. His presence was consistent and powerful, like a moon pushing and pulling the oceans in an everyday way. In the many hours I would spend in his workshop, Sam's nonchalant talk of "Strad"—or, for variation, "the old guy"—would sometimes make it seem that Stradivari was working still. In a way, Sam was Strad's apprentice, and the old guy might as well have been there in the shop each day, scraping away at a fiddle and muttering to himself in Italian.

The more I thought about Sam's situation, the more remarkable it seemed. His occupation appeared to refute one of the very basic rules of our culture: that science and technology keep making things better. In a world of billion-dollar search engines, phones that play movies, bioengineering and string theory, a shop in Brooklyn can still strive to produce a product that matched a tool more than three hundred years old. Was it craftsmanship or alchemy?

By lunchtime that day—a European-style snack of cheeses, dense dark bread, and fruits shared with Dietmar and Wiltrud on a worn wooden table in the big, bright loft kitchen—Sam and I were settling on one project I could follow.

A few years before, he'd promised a new fiddle to Eugene Drucker, one of the founders of the Emerson String Quartet, a New York–based chamber group that a lot of critics and many classical music fans would argue was the best of the current generation.

Two members of the Emerson, cellist David Finckel and violinist Philip Setzer, were currently playing Zygmuntowicz instruments. They had learned of Sam's abilities a decade earlier when Drucker had purchased another Zygmuntowicz violin. The violinist never really warmed to that fiddle and eventually sold it. Drucker was now playing exclusively on a Stradivari made in Cremona in 1686. This was before Strad's so-called Golden Period, which began around 1700 (when the master was pushing sixty!), but still, it was a Stradivari.

Gene Drucker had admitted to Sam that his violin could be temperamental, particularly under the rigorous international touring schedule the Emerson maintained and the consequent climate variations. Plus, the instruments that Sam had built for Finckel and Setzer just seemed more powerful, and the trend in all music, even classical chamber music, was toward more volume and force.

"That might be a good instrument for you to watch me build," Sam told me. "Gene is a very, very good player. And he's really sensitive to sound. And he plays on a Strad now. So my ultimate goal is to make him give up the Strad and play my instrument. The other two guys in the Emerson gave up their old instruments almost immediately. But they weren't playing Strads.

"Gene's Strad is an early—almost Amati-like—Strad," Sam explained. The young Antonio Stradivari was an apprentice in Nicolò Amati's workshop. "When it's playing well it's really something. The first time he ever came out here and played it for me I just said, 'What do you want from me? You sound absolutely fabulous.'

"But then he came out again and for whatever reason the Strad was not in good mettle and I could see what was bothering him. It wasn't like he told me anything specific, like he needed a dark sound or a light sound. It was more like a feel—what he needed the violin to do for him and what his musical struggles are. From that feeling I'm trying to surmise what to do. I wouldn't mind more information, but I think I have a free hand to just make a really good fiddle. And if I think it's really good, then he'll probably think it's really good, too."

Yes, this did seem like a perfect case study for building the magical box.

We finished lunch and cleared the table, and I told Sam I'd get out of his way so he could get some work done that day. On a last look around the workshop before I headed back to Manhattan, I noticed a button that Sam had stuck near the corner of his workbench. He'd had it made as a joke—but not completely a joke—to bring to a gathering of violin makers a few years before. It read:

STRAD MADE *NEW* FIDDLES.

Chapter 3

THE OLD GUY

*D*id I tell you about Strad's will?" Sam asked me. We were in his studio on a gray early fall afternoon, and he was seated on the rolling office chair at his workbench. Just back from a long vacation in Italy, he was cleaning up the odds and ends of his work schedule, getting ready to begin the Drucker violin. He'd been carving the arching of the spruce belly of another fiddle before I'd arrived, and there was a half-moon ridge of curly wood shavings around him, and the room smelled of dusty pine.

"It's kind of a riot. Strad's like some old man trying to fix everyone's wagon. He was a controlling patriarch his whole life. His children never really moved out. His good son, Francesco—he leaves everything to him. His bad son, Omobono, who Strad once tried to set up in business in Naples and who blew some money down there—*his* legacy is that his father forgives the debt that Omobono owes him. I mean, it would probably be hard to say that he was a nice person.

"But it stands to reason," Sam said, brushing a pile of shavings onto the floor. "Someone who is too nice of a person would not maintain that standard of quality and output for so many years. Stradivari was an analytic and controlling personality in everything he did. There's very little that's accidental in Strad's work. I know one of his violins—it's got a handwritten label in it that says *'Made by me at age 91.'* Like he was saying: *I can still do it!*"

It is no wonder that so many myths have grown around Stradivari, for so little is actually known of his life.

The historians have pinned down some facts, but not without pushing through a thicket of misapprehensions, and searching in vain over the centuries for documents and certitude. Stradivari's last will and testament was a recent discovery, stumbled upon in 1990 by a patient Italian violin expert named Carlo Chiesa while paging through musty church records in Cremona. Prior to that, all the documentation anyone had to go on was a bill for his first wife's funeral (the amount of which implied that the old guy had achieved a comfortable life; it is believed that there was a saying around Cremona at the time: "As rich as Stradivari") and a few letters to clients, one apologizing for being late in delivery. But if he was the greatest violin maker of all time, Stradivari never wrote down any of his secrets (judging from the misspellings in the few documents available, he wasn't very well educated), and nobody who knew him bothered to either. His last apprentice, Carlo Bergonzi, might have been an important link, but he died two years after the master. Stradivari's last surviving son, Paolo, didn't take up the trade and sold off the entire contents of his father's workshop—fiddles, forms, tools, templates—more than two hundred years ago. Some of the stuff has been brought back to a small museum dedicated to Stradivari in Cremona.

The standard study of Stradivari was published in 1902 in London, the work of three brothers—William Henry, Arthur, and Alfred Hill—from a long-established and respected family of luthiers and musicians. It is still in print. It is a sober, reasoned, and totally informed treatise, in many ways the opposite of Heron-Allen's amateur musings. By the time the Hills were putting together their magisterial study in the late 1800s they had seen and sometimes worked on many of the six hundred Stradivari instruments known at the time. But while the instruments survived, such seemingly simple documentation—like Stradivari's birth certificate—have been lost (or stolen as the Hills suspect), and even the great master's remains have been desecrated and scattered.

Antonio Stradivari (he often Latinized his name to Antonius Stradivarius, which was the style at the time) was probably born in 1644. Even that small fact is tentative and has been established by reverse reasoning, because the crotchety old patriarch insisted on writing his age on the labels of his later violins. This seemingly simple deduction has been challenged by at least one expert, who said those late labels were tampered with after Stradivari died. Renzo Bachetta edited the diary of Count Cozio di Salabue, perhaps the greatest violin collector of all time and the man who'd bought all of the master's workshop materials from his last surviving son. Bachetta discovered that the count admitted to adding age notations to some Stradivari fiddles he owned. Bachetta went as far as to publish an essay entitled "Stradivari Was Not Born in 1644." He thought that Antonio was born in 1648. Whatever the facts, the tenacious quality of the debate gives us clear clues to the passion people have about the Maestro of Cremona.

There is plenty of historical evidence that the Po Valley of Lombardy was not then the pleasant, fertile farm region it is now. In the early decades of the seventeenth century there was widespread famine, plague, and war. The Hills speculate that while the Stradivari family had been established in Cremona for hundreds of years, Antonio was actually born outside Cremona because his parents had fled the town, chased by either impending starvation, disease, or an encroaching army. The region spent much of that century under control of the Spanish crown, whose occupation was succeeded by the French and later Austrians.

Antonio returned to Cremona sometime in his boyhood; at some point between the ages of twelve and fourteen he became an apprentice in the shop of Nicolò Amati, son of one of the widely acknowledged inventors of the art of violin making and the most esteemed luthier of that century. Or, young Antonio might have been an apprentice wood-carver in the shop of an architect named Francesco Pescaroli, and switched to violin making as an adult. That's another debate among the experts.

Whichever is true, nobody knows *why* Stradivari was drawn to violin making, or even why, if it were not his decision, his family would force him into it. Less is known about his family, but it is nearly certain that none of his forebears had made violins, and primogeniture would be the obvious and natural reason for choosing the career in those days. There has been speculation that Amati was Antonio's godfather, but it has never been proven.

Could it be that the young Antonio was somehow compelled to construct the means of music? That he found himself, say, pulling reeds from the riverbank and carving flutes, as Sam Zygmuntowicz did centuries later as a boy in Philadelphia? Or was it a practical matter of his family not needing another mouth to feed? Or, if you believe the theory that he came to the craft relatively late—after learning to handle wood tools and inlay cabinetry—was the career switch because he longed to build objects that would be the tools of art rather than the mere repositories of coats and blankets?

Once you get started down this road to conjecture, it's easy to understand why lack of fact has spawned a bookshelf worth of fanciful speculation. We like to think of genius as directly linked with a colorful personality, and there's something unsatisfying in the thought that such exalted talent could reside in a dull and seemingly compulsive worker. In the town where he lived, Stradivari was actually fairly well known during his lifetime. There are notes of a Cremonese monk named Arisi that testify to that fact. His fame spread in the narrow world of music, and he was commissioned by foreign kings to make instruments for the court. But after Stradivari died, his reputation faded quickly. It took nearly a century after his death for his mastery to be rediscovered, and buoyed by the tendencies of the Romantic movement, his reputation reached its apogee, it seems, in the last decades of the nineteenth century.

The library I use, the New York Public, holds fifty-five volumes devoted to Antonio Stradivari. Five are categorized as novels and eight are listed as fiction for young people. The rest broadly fall into either technical analyses of the master's craft or richly illustrated portfolios of instruments that survive. Every writer is constrained by the same paucity of fact, and the more recent have to distill what little verifiable truth there is from a cauldron of sentimental myth. "Over time a vast hagiography dedicated to the master Cremonese violin maker was introduced," writes the contemporary Cremonese violin maker Carlo Bissolotti, "which caused even further confusion and enveloped the craftsman in a thick fog of obscurity."

Maybe, as the Hills concluded, Stradivari simply had a quiet and happy life, evidenced by his long and fruitful productivity. Certainly what little biographical interpretation the Hill brothers offered in their study approached the level of hagiography. But it seems there just was something in the Victorian air that made Stradivari irresistible as a Romantic icon. In 1873, George Eliot was compelled to write a poem called "Stradivarius." It includes this stanza.

> *That plain white-aproned man who stood at work*
> *Patient and accurate full fourscore years,*
> *Cherished his sight and touch by temperance,*
> *And since keen sense is love of perfectness*
> *Made perfect violins, the needed paths*
> *For inspiration and high mastery.*

Only a few years later, when Edward Heron-Allen was publishing his examination of violin making, he chose as the book's frontispiece that poem by Henry Wadsworth Longfellow:

> *The Instrument on which he played*
> *Was in Cremona's workshops made*
> *... Perfect in each minutest part,*
> *A marvel of the lutist's art;*
> *And in the hollow chamber, thus*
> *The maker from whose hands it came*
> *Had written his unrivalled name—*
> *"Antonius Stradivarius."*

Among a certain class on the island of the Virgin Queen, an Italian workman more than a hundred years dead was developing something of a cult. It continues still with surprising strength.

Nowadays we'll see advertisements in which an old

fiddle is placed next to an overpriced watch or an aged bottle of booze and we're expected to make the association of quality. There's a line of crystal and silver named for Stradivari. When a young trumpeter decides to buy a serious instrument that could carry him into professional status, chances are good it will be called a "Stradivarius," though it was stamped out in a factory in the decidedly unromantic town of Elkhart, Indiana. I own three. The top journal of the string playing world is simply called *The Strad*.

Many people know just enough of Stradivari's reputation that when they find an old fiddle in the attic with a Stradivari label inside they think he is going to make them suddenly rich. Not long after I started learning about violin making, I met a former network newsman at a party. He was a smart and sober-seeming fellow, but when he told me of the violin a dead relative had left him I could almost see the cartoon dollar signs appear in his eyes. I had to break it to him that so many thousands of cheap, mass-produced fiddles have been made over the years and had a label with the name Antonius Stradivarius stuck inside that most violin dealers have a firmly discouraging form letter to send would-be millionaires who have found a dusty violin case in an attic.

But Strad's reputation, both real and imagined, has enormous staying power. As recently as 1991, the Pulitzer Prize–winning novelist John Hersey was bitten by the Stradivari bug and published a novel called *Antonietta*, in which he takes the basic facts available and builds a sentimental portrait of a love-struck craftsman, a widower, who woos his second wife by building her one of those perfect fiddles that George Eliot rhapsodized about. Hersey was the clear-eyed and meticulous writer who gave us the masterpiece of reporting called *Hiroshima*, yet when he encountered the legend of Stradivari it was the myth that captivated his imagination.

In this century there have been two biographical films devoted to Stradivari, one made in Germany in 1935 and another produced for Italian television in 1989 starring Anthony Quinn. How many late Renaissance craftsmen have *one* movie made about their life? Since Hersey's book was published, a Canadian filmmaker named François Girard became even more besotted with the Stradivari of legend. The 1998 movie *The Red Violin* follows an instrument through centuries as it is passed from owner to owner and from continent to continent. In the first segment of the film, the violin is made by a Cremonese master, who uses the blood of his dead wife to color the varnish of a fiddle that is fated to become famous. The violin maker character is called Bussotti, but could this be anybody other than Stradivari?

There is at least one other great designer and craftsman whose name is as well known as Stradivari's, a man who also took wood and made art. But no casting director has ever had to wonder what actor to get to play the part of Thomas Chippendale.

Sam Zygmuntowicz brings a set of interests beyond biography to his studies of Stradivari. While he is amused by something like the discovery of the old man's will and the unavoidable glimpse into the craftsman's character, Sam would rather that the master had bequeathed to posterity some technical treatise. "What I want," he says, "and I suppose what most violin makers would want, is a little handbook that would say, for instance, 'If you want to make your instrument more powerful in the upper register, try making it thicker here, here, and here.'" If Antonio Stradivari had left behind his shop notes, as the neophyte Edward Heron-Allen did, he might have explained some things that still perplex people. For example, why, one day in middle age, when his technical skills were at their height, did he change the size of the form on which he built his fiddles?

Working in the shop of Nicolò Amati, Stradivari no doubt assumed the normal duties of an apprentice, duties that grew in complexity and importance as his skill increased. By tradition, an apprentice could at a certain point begin making violins that bore his own label. The earliest Stradivari label ever discovered is dated 1666, when he would have been either twenty-two or eighteen, depending on which set of speculations you believe on his birth date. Though he set up his own shop in 1670, Stradivari spent the next two decades producing instruments very much like those of Amati—so much so that experts call this his "Amatise" period. It was obvious that Antonio possessed a prodigious talent. As the Hills say, the finish work on his instruments "marks him as having been one of the most dexterous craftsmen the world has ever known." But to that point he played it safe as a designer.

The forms were virtually the same as those he'd used in his master's shop, the details were similar, the varnish retained Amati's characteristic yellow tint.

Then, in 1690, Stradivari changed the length of his fiddles. The change was—about a quarter of an inch! In the world of violins, that amount is huge. But to the rest of us ... well. For comparison, the case that holds a compact disc is much thicker—about three-eighths of an inch. I pulled the contents of my wallet—two credit cards, a driver's license, and another card with a magnetic strip that gets me on the subway—and stacked them. That was almost a quarter of an inch. When I added a business card it was too much. For violin experts, this alteration by Stradivari ranks in the same category as the day Picasso decided, *What the hell, I'll put the two eyes on the same side of the nose.*

Of course, there can only be speculation—and plenty of it—about what he was after. Maybe he was impressed by the bigger fiddles of a maker from the nearby town of Brescia, Giovanni Maggini. Perhaps Stradivari had a premonition that the sonic requirements of violins would change and followed the simple notion that a bigger size would mean a bigger sound. (Which is not really the case, it turns out.) Or, could it be that he finally had to throw off the yoke of Amati for good and produce a violin that would be obviously his own?

Stradivari produced the longer fiddle almost exclusively for about eight years. Then, just as mysteriously, he went back to the old, smaller forms. As the seventeenth century was about to end, he was a middle-aged man (by today's standards) who'd been working at his craft for forty years. Did men have midlife crises then? Was it, as John Hersey imagined, that his first wife was gone (Signora Francesca Feraboschi Stradivari was buried on May 25, 1698, and it cost her bereaved husband 182 lira to pay for various clergy and professional mourners) and the old guy had found someone new and was in love again?

Whatever caused the change, Antonio Stradivari, as the century changed, was about to go from making extraordinary violins to making perfect violins.

Chapter 4

THE VIOLINIST

"I only started to play the violin when I was eight and a half," says Eugene Drucker. "Compared to some people, it was late.

"I played the piano a little bit when I was five. My mother played the piano, though she wasn't really a professional. Music was certainly held in high esteem in my family.

"My father was a violinist for the Metropolitan Opera for many years. He had played with the Busch Quartet, which was a famous quartet, for a few years after World War II. I think that in the late 1950s, before I started to play the violin, it was a tough life for most orchestral musicians. The pay wasn't as good as it is now. The musicians didn't get much time off. I think the general idea amongst musicians was, 'Don't make your kids become musicians.' So I think that's why my father didn't push me. But once I started and he realized I had some talent, then he became very interested.

"My father was my teacher at the very beginning. And I had another teacher, a Viennese woman named Renée Hurtig, who was the sister of Felix Galimir, who had a famous quartet, the Galimir Quartet. Renée was a very good teacher—a very caring person with a lot of integrity—and gave me a solid foundation.

"I wouldn't say that I knew right away that I was going to be a professional musician. I was very affected by the Kennedy assassination when I was around eleven or twelve. I had this notion that I would go into law and politics. It certainly wasn't serious; it was a fantasy, really. Then in the tenth grade I got into the High School of Music and Art, and after that it was pretty clear to me—I was thirteen—that I was going to become a musician."

More than thirty-five years have gone by since Gene Drucker chose the course of his life. In that time, he'd graduated from the nation's most prestigious music conservatory, Juilliard, *and* a premier Ivy League school, Columbia, where he earned a bachelor's degree in literature. He'd been a founding member of the Emerson String Quartet and with that group had already won six Grammy Awards. He'd traveled all over the world and performed at the most famous concert halls. And still, from everything I'd heard about him, as I approached his apartment building on West End Avenue in upper Manhattan, I expected to meet someone who was a classic Upper West

Side type. I'm not big on puns, but there was no avoiding this one: Drucker, I assumed, would be high-strung.

Before I contacted Gene to see if he'd be willing to let me follow the process of building the new violin he'd commissioned, I was cautioned with a warning from Sam Zygmuntowicz: "He's very sensitive."

When I first talked with him on the phone, Drucker said that he'd be willing to discuss why he wanted a new violin, even though he owned a Stradivari, and he'd be happy to let me follow the process as he tried to adopt a new fiddle. "There's just one request I'd like to make," Drucker said jokingly. "That you'll try not to make me seem as neurotic as I really am."

At our first meeting, Drucker seemed a little wary, but relaxed and awfully smart, with a quick and subtle sense of humor. He is very slim and handsome in a way that seems old-fashioned, like someone out of the Roaring Twenties, with curly black hair and soulful dark eyes. He met me in the lobby of the huge brick-and-stone apartment building where he lives with his wife, Roberta, a professional cellist he'd met on a chamber orchestra gig; and their son, Julian.

"There's a Tibetan restaurant near here that I like," Drucker said. "Would that be all right with you? I'm a vegetarian and they have good vegetarian dishes. I try to go there when I can. My son doesn't like that kind of food." We strolled a few blocks on a bright, perfect summer day and got a table. I set up a tape recorder to capture the conversation as we both ate, something I've done dozens of times over the years with all sorts of people, including some well-known writers and broadcasters, folks who make their living with words. Often, when I listen to a tape later, both my guest and myself are so inarticulate that it seems English is not our first language. With Gene Drucker well-chosen words formed sentences and those became logical paragraphs. He was perhaps the most articulate person I've ever interviewed. I asked him why he'd ordered a violin from Sam Zygmuntowicz, started into my tofu, and didn't say another word for quite a while.

"There's an incentive for me to get a Zygmuntowicz instrument," Gene began, "because there are already two members of my quartet who play Sam's instruments who are so happy with them, and I can see and hear what it has done for their playing. My wife also has one of his cellos and likes it very much.

"Our cellist, David Finckel, had a Guadagnini[1] cello. His had a very beautiful sound, but it was not in particularly good condition. He got a really soulful sound out of it, but it didn't have the really big, bassy quality. I think when he got the new instrument from Sam it gave him certain dynamics that he wasn't getting from the Guadagnini. Of course, instruments change as you play them. Sometimes David's *new* cello sounded more like an old Italian instrument; sometimes it sounded more like a modern instrument. When the Zygmuntowicz is sounding its best it's extraordinary.

"But I had a theory. It seemed to me that some of the

---

[1] Guadagnini was a late contemporary of Stradivari who was long (and wrongly) thought to have been an apprentice of the master. He died in 1786, one of the last of the great violin makers of the period.

pitfalls of modern instruments would be less for cellos than violins. There's a characteristic of modern violins I haven't been able to take to, which is a certain shrillness. Maybe that's even the way Stradivari's instruments sounded when they were first made. When they mellow over the years, if they're fine instruments, they develop depth and roundness but retain some brilliance as well. I hadn't seen that yet in a modern violin. So I figured that it was easier to do that with a cello than with a violin.

"But then Phil Setzer, our other violinist, got his violin from Sam. He had played a Lupot[2] before that and the new instrument was a big improvement for him. It belied my stereotype—it wasn't shrill."

The violin and viola are unique among musical instruments in the way the player hears them. For instance, when I play the trumpet, the sound emanates from the bell, which is about two feet in front of my face, and projects outward. Woodwinds aren't quite so projecting. Their players are more enveloped in the sound, but usually it emanates at some distance from their ears. Even cellos and bass fiddles have a center of sound that starts at the musician's midsection.

But with the violin, the first wave of the sound, from the bow scraping across the string to the burst of melody out of the wooden box, is a few inches below the player's left ear. The degree of immediacy and intimacy is very high. All musicians operate constantly in a complicated

---

[2] Lupot worked in Paris in the nineteenth century and was strongly influenced by the rediscovery of Stradivari's work after nearly a century of obscurity.

feedback loop, their trained muscles making a sound, their ears hearing that sound and their brain analyzing the quality—fullness, pitch, timing, emotion—and then telling the muscles to make minute adjustments to keep it up, or change it a little. With violinists, this process is exaggerated by the output being so close to the input. There's a phrase for the phenomenon: *what you hear under your ear.* "I am very finicky about what I hear under my ear," Gene Drucker said. "It could be that I'm more focused on what I hear there than most players." He told me that as he has aged, his hearing has changed and made matters even more complicated.

"I've gotten more sensitive—even *hyper*sensitive—to certain frequencies. Anything that sounds metallic under my ears—to me that's a negative word. I can't stand too much surface noise, anything that doesn't sound like the deep core of the tone. I want power and beauty, and I'm very reactive to anything that I don't consider beautiful."

What he talked about for the next half hour made me understand why Gene was worried that he might seem neurotic. He ate slowly and fitfully, moving food around the plate with his chopsticks, and told me in great detail how he'd come to decide what type of strings to use on his fiddle. And how, while other members of the Emerson Quartet liked to play on new strings, he had trouble dealing with the breaking-in period and preferred old strings. He analyzed why he was never able to use a shoulder rest on the violin, as many players do. Then he explored the subject of why he'd never adopted the habit of using at least a handkerchief or cloth to cover the chin rest of the violin for some cushioning and to counteract the wear on the neck from hours and hours of playing. He dissected the process by which he achieves proper vibrato on his instrument, taking into account the size and springiness of his fingertips and the moisture content of his skin.

"The other guys in the quartet think I'm crazy," Drucker said. "And I probably am. For example, I don't want to get my fingers dirty right before I play, because that means I have to wash my hands, and if I wash my hands I feel like my fingers on the strings don't have any traction.

"Phil Setzer, for example—his skin is much oilier than mine, so he has to wash his hands. He's always washing his hands before we play. But, of course, I'm the one who comes off looking like he's crazy, because if it's right before a performance or during a lunch break in a recording session, sometimes I'll put my left hand under my leg while I eat so it won't get dirty.

"They laugh at me and I know it's funny and ridiculous. I can say to myself that these are small and silly things, yet time and time again I have to deal with consequences if I don't do things according to the prescribed rituals that I have."

Those of us who play brass instruments often suspect that fiddle players regard us as the Neanderthals of the orchestra. And, in response, we dismiss violinists as being rather effete. I remember a teacher of mine once saying rather scornfully, "Those fiddle players think they can hear the grass grow." As I listened to Gene Drucker I began to realize that the level of intimacy he had with his instrument was simply deeper than I had experienced, perhaps deeper than I could imagine. But the detail of his concerns also made me empathize with the other members of the Emerson Quartet. And I remembered something Sam had told me. "I've never had a lot of trouble with my clients," he'd said. "But Gene could be tricky."

To bring the talk back more squarely on the actual violin, I asked Drucker to tell me how he'd come to own a Stradivari and how important it was to play on a good instrument. I picked up my chopsticks and figured I could finish lunch without needing to say another word.

"I always wanted a fine Italian violin," Gene began. "I never felt that it had to be a Strad just because he was the most famous Italian violin maker.

"My first instrument was a Fawick—Thomas Fawick. He was an industrialist of some kind and a music lover who actually commissioned makers in France—I think in Mirecourt—to build instruments, and then he would put his label in them. My father was playing a Guadagnini. It was in pristine condition, just amazing condition. He was frustrated with it because it had a bright soprano sound but not enough depth. So he sold it and bought a Guarneri—not a del Gesù, a Joseph filius Andreae.[3]

"By then we were starting to overlap. I was sixteen and getting pretty advanced. But when my father bought the Italian violin I didn't want to play it at first. I felt, 'Let me take another year and hone my skills more on the Fa-

---

[3] In the Guarneri family of violin makers, Giuseppe, the father of the man who became known as "del Gesù," signed his fiddles in tribute to *his* father, "son of Andrea."

wick.' Which is what I did. Only rarely did I allow myself the privilege of playing on that Guarneri. I was very good at deferment of gratification—much more then than I am now. But after a while I was playing the Guarneri more than my father was."

Whatever the teenage Drucker was doing, it was working. He was made assistant concertmaster of the top Juilliard orchestra when he was seventeen and served as sole concertmaster in the two years before he graduated. During the summer breaks from Juilliard and Columbia, he studied on a fellowship at the Tanglewood Institute in Massachusetts. He was certainly on a track to land a job with a top orchestra after graduation, but he began to gravitate toward chamber music and the solo repertoire. After five years of college, at age twenty-one, he received a diploma from Juilliard and a BA from Columbia and started entering solo violin competitions. He was a prizewinner in several. He also began performing at the Marlboro Festival, one of the country's top chamber music programs. In 1976, Gene and some friends from Juilliard started a string quartet. It was the year of the Bicentennial, and looking for a quintessentially American name, they called it the Emerson, after the writer and Transcendentalist philosopher Ralph Waldo Emerson. Within a decade the Emerson had become, arguably, the most successful young quartet in the world.

"I was fairly happy in those days with the Guarneri," Drucker remembered. "I knew that it was not necessarily the instrument for the rest of my life. It wasn't the most powerful instrument, but it had a penetrating sound.

Frankly, I didn't attach as much importance to sound then. I was more involved in other elements of playing. I was probably more concerned with clarity, clean playing, playing well in tune, articulation. The Guarneri gave me all that. Maybe I should have paid more attention to sound.

"Anyway, eventually I came under a lot of pressure from the other guys in the group to lose the Guarneri. They didn't like it. They knew I had a very good trade-in value with that instrument and they pressured me to sell it. It was sort of a sore spot between me and them.

"I never thought I could own a Strad. Partly, because my father bought the Guarneri privately, instead of through a dealer, the value had increased by ten times in fifteen years. Over the years, Jacques Français[*] always had commented how much he liked the Guarneri, and he was true to his word and gave me a good trade-in. I still had to come up with a considerable amount of cash in addition to that."

It was in 1983 that Drucker traded in his Joseph filius Andrea Guarneri and bought a 1686 Stradivari called the Rosgonyl, after a Hungarian violinist who'd owned it early in the twentieth century. Not long before Gene got the fiddle, it had belonged to an assistant concertmaster in the New York Philharmonic named Frank Gullino. There is a story that one night while playing a concerto with the Philharmonic, Isaac Stern broke a string on his

---

[*] Français was from a family of French violin makers and dealers. He emigrated and set up shop in New York. His partner was Sam Zygmuntowicz's mentor, the restoration expert René Morel.

famous Guarneri del Gesù and Gullino quickly handed over the Rosgonyl so the star could complete the performance. The Rosgonyl sounded just as good as the Panette, according to the tale Drucker heard.

Drucker paid about $250,000 for the Rosgonyl. On the day we met, he wasn't sure of its current market value, though he was paying insurance premiums on a policy for $1.5 million.

You would think that an object worth that much might come with some sort of guarantee that it would be trouble-free, but Gene had learned in the twenty years he'd owned the Stradivari that what the Hill brothers called "ne plus ultra" was hardly no-hassle.

"I loved the Strad," Gene said. "It took me a while to find the right bow for it. Over a few years I think I tried sixty or seventy different bows. After about four years I finally found the right one. When it was sounding right, the instrument had an amazing vocal quality."

The problem was, the instrument wasn't always sounding right, and, ironically, its problems were magnified as the Emerson and Drucker achieved greater and greater success. Stradivari somehow built instruments that have set the level of quality for the ages, but he could never have imagined the demands a modern musician would make on an instrument. As the Emerson began recording for the Deutsche Grammophon label, its players were put under the microscopic scrutiny of sophisticated microphones and advanced digital recorders, where every flaw was magnified. And as the quartet's reputation increased, so did their complicated and busy touring schedule; the strains of international travel taxed the old instrument even more.

"I had some real trouble in Aspen," Gene said. The Emerson had been longtime participants in the Aspen Music Festival, one of the great summer classical music festivals in America. In 1994, the group began recording the complete string quartets of Dimitry Shostakovich during their residency in Colorado. (It later earned the group two Grammys.) There was a pause in the project for several years and then it picked up again in 1998, by which time the recording equipment had gotten almost exponentially more sophisticated. At the same time, Gene's Stradivari got temperamental, reacting to the quick trip from the humid New York City summer to the dry western mountains.

"It was a real struggle," Gene remembered. "The fiddle went from sounding fantastic to sounding a way I couldn't deal with too well emotionally. It was choking up. This kind of inconsistency made me very frustrated." He made an emergency visit to a violin repair shop in Aspen and had the instrument adjusted, a process where a small wooden peg, called the sound post, which is wedged inside the violin box, is moved by minute degrees. That move affects the tension of the strings and alters the entire feedback loop of the way the instrument feels to play and, consequently, how it sounds. All violinists must have their instruments adjusted regularly, but it is a standing joke in the Emerson Quartet and among the small coterie of New York chamber music players that Gene Drucker has more adjustments than anyone. He swears that is a myth. Whatever the case, Drucker would usually entrust the process only to René Morel. The emergency adjustment in Colorado got him through the recording session but may have been the first glimmer that he needed to commission a new instrument from Sam Zygmuntowicz.

"Sam and I discussed making a copy of my Strad briefly," Gene told me, "and decided there really wasn't much point in doing that." Phil Setzer's Zygmuntowicz was modeled on the Stradivari that belonged to one of the last great soloists-turned-teachers, Oscar Shumsky, who taught both Setzer and Drucker at Juilliard.

"I love the way Phil sounds on his instrument, but when I pick it up and play it, it doesn't feel right," Gene said. "I knew Sam had made copies of other great Strads. Sam actually made measurements of my Strad. I think he could hear what it was I loved in the Strad. And he could also see some of the things that frustrate me too." When Gene visited the shop in Brooklyn, he played several of Sam's instruments and gravitated toward models that were based on the designs of Guarneri del Gesù.

"I tried two Guarneri models that he had in the shop," Gene said, "and I wanted a sort of fusion of the two. I took to those instruments very quickly. A few times I've had the good fortune to put my hands on a Guarneri del Gesù. Most of them were just amazing. There's a reason that they're the most expensive violins in existence. They are very powerful but they have this depth and a dark, robust sound. I have to say that my Strad has a darker sound than most Strads. So in that sense, maybe it reflects some of my preferences.

"But all these words become rather limited when you really try to imagine the sound characteristics of different instruments. We only have a few words to describe the sound of an instrument, and the gradations are far more numerous than the words we have to describe them."

Listening to Gene made me realize the difficulty inherent in a successful transaction between a luthier and a violinist. There was goodwill on both sides, of course; both men wanted a great-sounding new violin. But there seemed to be huge potential for misunderstanding.

"I don't know exactly what effect the new violin is going to have on me individually or on the group," Gene said. "I suppose it's going to be similar to what happened when Sam's other instruments came into the group. The sound will be more powerful and clearer.

"I'm just going to wait and see. I don't want to make Sam nervous. I'm sure it's going to be a fine instrument. It's just that it may be a little harder to please me than it was for Phil and David, because neither of them was playing a Stradivari. I have to say that no matter how much trouble I sometimes have with my Strad, the kind of up-and-down relationship I have with it, it's still one of the best early Strads and Stradivari is still the greatest violin maker who ever lived.

"It's going to be harder for me to say, 'I don't need that anymore.' The soul nourishment it has given me over the years is great. I've been playing it for nearly twenty years now and it is so very much a part of my identity."

Chapter 5

THE SINGING TREE

*G*iven, a log of wood.

Make a fiddle.

Trouble is, there really are no givens in violin making.

After we both returned to New York from Oberlin, I began to call Sam regularly and invite myself to Brooklyn for visits. He kept assuring me that he was going to get started on the fiddle for Gene Drucker anytime now. There were a few odds and ends to clear off his workbench. And it was summer, and, as might be expected of anyone who thinks of himself as only a demi-American, Sam was following the European ethos and planning a long vacation. In this case, off to Italy to visit his wife's relatives in the northern lake region. And maybe a side trip to a wood dealer near Brescia, just about an hour's train ride from Stradivari's home, Cremona.

Good-tone wood for a high-end fiddle doesn't exactly fall from trees. And choosing the right wood is the crucial first step in building a new instrument. "There are decisions I have to make first that will predetermine the quality of the instrument," Sam told me. "The character of the wood will definitely predispose the character of the sound. The nature of the fiddle is in its materials."

Two kinds of wood are used predominately—spruce for the belly, or sound board, and maple for the back. Both are quite common, but coming up with the perfect raw material is nearly as much of an art as the careful carving that will follow. In 1866, the top violin maker of the day, Jean-Baptiste Vuillame, wrote to a client, "If you could see the bother I have and the lengths I go through to find the right materials for my violins." Times haven't changed.

One day I arrived at his studio and asked Sam to show me his wood supply. I'd seen one violin expert compare the experience to visiting the wine cellar of an oenophile. Sam put down a fiddle he was repairing and said to follow him. We headed out of the workshop and down the hall toward the kitchen.

Past the big commercial stove was a short, dark hallway leading to a bathroom. One wall was lined with simple wood-framed shelves that climbed from the floor all the way to the high ceilings. On those shelves rested what appeared to be hundreds of pieces of wood, looking like a very large and eccentric collection of children's blocks.

Sam led me over to the shelves and gave them a proprietary look. With a small sweeping gesture he said, "I've spent thousands of dollars on this stuff. There's forty or fifty thousand dollars here—probably more than that." He reached into the stacks and moved a few pieces, in the way someone would shift books while searching on a library shelf. "Probably," he said, "like many violin makers I will end my life with some of the best pieces of wood sitting here gathering dust. I've told my wife that after I'm gone a lot of handsome young violin makers would do almost anything to get their hands on this wood."

I asked Sam how he picks a piece from all these when he's starting to build a violin.

He reached up and pulled a thin triangle of wood from the shelf. Held between his hands, it looked like a very wide shingle of clapboard siding for a house, though it was less than two feet in length. Sam rubbed the wood.

"You can tell a lot about the wood just by running your hands over it," he said. "You hear that little hiss? This is tone wood, so it has to make a sound. It's spruce, which is used in almost all stringed instruments as the soundboard. Pianos, guitars, mandolins, fiddles—it's the universal choice. That's because it happens to be the strongest wood per unit of weight. It's very light but very strong. They also make masts for ships with it."

Sam pushed the piece of spruce toward me and into better light. Close up, I could see thin bands of dark wood alternating with broader bands of light wood, almost like a corduroy. "There's an alternation between summer and winter growth in a conifer tree like spruce," he told me. "It grows fast in the summer and then slows down in the fall and virtually stops in winter. Functionally, those broad bands of lighter wood are very light, but they're reinforced by the very hard bands of darker wood. It's kind of why corrugated cardboard is so strong, or the beams in a ceiling with air space in between, or the rebar in concrete. Spruce is naturally engineered to create the same structure."

The particular piece he has handed me was sawn on what is called a quarter cut, taken out of the spruce log like a piece of pie. Usually, two of these pieces would be joined together at the thick ends to make a violin belly, which, in finished form, is no more than ten inches wide, fourteen inches long, and only four centimeters at its thickest—half that in many places. A pie cut of wood like this could cost anywhere from fifty dollars well into the hundreds. Factors that affect the cost include age, quality of the cut, pedigree, and what the violin maker is willing to pay.

"This stuff is really old," Sam told me. "It came from a shop in Paris that was run by Jacques Français's father, Emile. So I know it's at least eighty years old, and probably older. I spent a bloody fortune for it, and some of it has been disappointing. But you look at a piece like this and you just say, WOW! It's as old as the hills and it's split well. I'm pretty sure the belly of the fiddle I'll make for Gene will come from this stock."

For the violin's back, maple is the standard. The back is not quite so vital to sound production as the belly, but it is very important for the look of the fiddle. The natural flamelike design in maple can be hypnotically beautiful. "Imagine a woman with curly hair," Sam said, "and imagine setting her hair with epoxy and then grinding off the ends, cutting across all those layers of fibers. Great-looking maple, when you turn it, catches the light in different ways. Some grains absorb the light, some reflect it. And when you turn it again it shifts."

It seems that from the very beginning of violin making, luthiers have been looking for a piece of wood to make them say WOW! Making a magical box requires at least a little sorcery. Among the many tangled tales that have been told about the "secrets" of the great makers of Cremona, the nature and handling of the wood ranks second as a subject of speculation. Only the varnish on that wood has inspired more conjecture, suspicion, and downright superstition. Perhaps it's coincidental that picking the wood is the first job in building a fiddle, and varnishing is the last.

Almost any kind of wood *could* be used to make a violin. A captured American flier fashioned a fiddle from beech bed slats in a World War II German prison camp. Pinchas Zukerman played that instrument once and claimed it sounded pretty good. But spruce and maple are by far the most common. Of course almost nothing is commonplace in lutherie, or without history and mystique.

Some think that the spruce must be from a high altitude and a bad soil—a tree that had to fight hard for its life is somehow better equipped to stand up to the stresses of music making. Some go as far as to recommend that one must only use the wood from the south side of trees that have grown on the south side of a hill. There is a whole school of speculation that Stradivari and Guarneri somehow "treated" their wood, and that is why their instruments are so glorious.

This speculation has a long history. I had found a copy of Edward Heron-Allen's strange little book, *Violin-Making as it was, and is*, and it had become my bedside table companion. He devoted a chapter to tone wood. It is characteristic of the book as a whole: peppered with Latin phrases, containing a thicket of footnotes that support an argument that is detailed and certain in its judgments. "The best maple to be had for our purpose," Heron-Allen wrote, "is that which grows on the southern slopes of the Carpathians." Elsewhere, he decided, "There is no proof in existence that the old Italians used any artificial means for drying or preparing their wood."

It wasn't long after Heron-Allen published his treatise that the Hills released their definitive study of Stradivari. Their combined expertise dwarfed that of the obsessive amateur, but they had to deal with the same wild theories of woodcutting and wood treatment. The Hills' sober and studied conclusion on the quality of Stradivari's wood was that he used better stuff when he was being paid more for an instrument, and that some years there was simply higher-quality wood to be had than others.

"The height of absurdity is reached," the Hills wrote, "when we are gravely informed by ... a German professor of violin ... that the secret of the unrivalled tone of Stradivari and of other fine instruments may be found in the fact that the bellies were made of 'Balsam Pine,' a wood which grew in Northern Italy at the period when those makers flourished, but has since gradually become extinct."

But the height of absurdity hadn't been fully reached back in the 1800s, at least not according to the violin makers I met in Oberlin. During one workshop I attended, the name Nagyvary came up, and there was a collective snicker. Joseph Nagyvary is a Hungarian who fled the Communist regime in that country when he was a student in the 1950s. He dreamed of becoming a professional violinist but ended up with degrees in chemistry and has been teaching biochemistry and biophysics for several decades at Texas A&M University in Waco. On the side, he makes his own fiddles and regularly posits new theories on what makes the great fiddles great.

In 1977 Nagyvary gave a presentation at the annual convention of the Violin Society of America, in which he said that his scientific studies led him to believe that the chemistry of the classic Cremonese instruments was as important as their design and workmanship. His theories dated back to his days as a student in Switzerland. Every summer he would take a vacation in Italy. When poking around the museums and old palaces of Lombardi, the province containing Cremona and Milan, he noticed that anything old and wooden had been riddled by woodworm. But not fiddles. He speculated that Stradivari and his contemporaries treated their wood with antipest chemicals. Studying tiny chips of old instruments under powerful microscopes, he found traces of borax (which served as an insecticide and made the wood harder and more brilliant sounding), gums from fruit trees (which helped to prevent mold), and crystal powders, which would be inedible to pests.

Nagyvary tried to convince modern violin makers to use these substances on their new violins to re-create the sound of Stradiviari, an achievement he continues to attempt himself.

Sam Zygmuntowicz confessed to me that he has tried wood treatments over the years but has come to the conclusion that they are not worth the trouble. He sticks to the principle that all good quality wood of a certain age will make a good violin, leaning away from the modern science of Nagyvary (whom Sam considers an eccentric who has some good ideas and would be better off if he didn't keep announcing he'd discovered "the secret") and toward the more commonsense approach of the Hill brothers.

That day, shuffling through the dusty stacks of his wood collection, I asked Sam if he had ever come across any extinct wood on his buying trips. He just shook his head and laughed. "Once wood is fifty years old it gets a little difficult to even say the exact age," he said. "That's because wood ages a little bit like a cheese, from the outside in. There's a stage where it's curing all the way through and you're getting real oxidation. It really changes something about the wood. If you look at a violin top that's been made with wood that's less than fifty years old you can see a little bit of light through it, like a lampshade. But really old wood—like Strads—all those fiddles are opaque.

And it's not because they're thicker; they're often thinner than newer fiddles. Something has oxidized within the wood and changed its nature in some way. It feels different. It smells different."

Sam let me feel and smell the spruce from Emile François that he was planning to use for the Drucker violin. The smell was mild and dusty, and the feel was almost sandy and much lighter than I expected. What about the maple back?

"When I was first starting out," Sam said, "there was this catalog put out by a wood dealer. He had all these categories—slightly flamed to very nicely flamed aged maple. There were eight categories, and each was more expensive than the last. And then there was a final category that you couldn't even buy through the catalog that was called 'Exhibition Piece Indeed!'

"I'd go to his place in Vermont and spend two days going through every piece of wood in his place. One day I saw that in the back there were these boxes that had some of these pieces in them and they were just gorgeous. And I asked him to sell me some, and he'd say, 'Oh, I'm saving those to pay for my kids' college education.'

"And then on one trip I bought four grand's worth of wood and I convinced him to sell me one of those maple pieces that was Exhibition Piece Indeed! So for Gene, the back will be Exhibition Piece Indeed!"

Sam began to place back the pieces of wood he'd drawn from the shelves. "I can make just as good fiddles out of really top-quality newish wood," he said. "Meaning ten years old. I've had fiddles that turned out really smashing with wood that was eight years old. It's the intrinsic quality of the wood that's important." He was slipping the old piece of spruce back into its slot. "I don't want to make a fetish out of old wood," he said. "You can really get seduced by really old wood. And you can make a bad fiddle with old wood if you're not careful.

"But, all other things being equal, older is better."

That idea would dog the rest of my days in the world of violins.

Chapter 6

TRADITION AND
THE INDIVIDUAL
TALENT

The design of the violin—those sensuous, feminine curves of shoulders, waist, and hips (Man Ray famously superimposed the instrument onto the back of a shapely woman)—is the result of a long-simmering stew of intellect, practicality, and even some mysticism. It has been thought that the violin's shape and workings were influenced by such varied forces as the geometries of Pythagoras, the transcendent theories of Plato, and the workbench savvy of Stradivari and his forbears. But the real reason a fiddle looks the way it does is simply because that's what works best—though no one really knows why.

"To many people a violin is a beautiful object," writes the Cambridge don Sir James Beament in his wonderful and witty treatise called *The Violin Explained*. "To a physicist it is a hideously complex shape."

A hundred years ago, Edward Heron-Allen, in his typical way, gave detailed and explicit instructions on how to design a violin outline using a ruler and compass (he admitted to borrowing the technique from an earlier work by Jacob Augustus Otto). The process involves starting with a perpendicular line as long as the violin will be, usually around fourteen inches. Then that line must be divided extremely carefully into seventy-two equal parts. Next, scribe twenty-four horizontal lines using certain of those seventy-two reference points. After that, the compass comes out and a series of arches must be drawn and it gets even more complicated. I tried one day to design a violin using Heron-Allen's technique and after a few hours had a piece of paper covered with straight lines and curved lines that looked like the plan for the worst highway interchange ever devised. Heron-Allen was operating in a day before the adjective *anal-retentive* was in the vocabulary, but it would be hard to imagine accomplishing this feat of draftsmanship without a prodigious gift for patience. Even the fussy author described the design technique as "terribly complicated" and conceded that it was practically unnecessary. Even in his day, perfectly good fiddle outlines based on the masterworks were readily available to him. It was pointless to start from scratch.

It is now more than four centuries since a lot of trial and

error produced this hideously complex, yet practically perfect, shape. A modern luthier like Sam Zygmuntowicz has any number of models to help him make that shape. Like almost all current makers, his favored exemplars are Stradivari and Guarneri. It is almost unheard of to mix models by the two dead Italians, though they worked contemporaneously in the same small town and followed a remarkably uniform tradition. Since the days when Sam worked to make nearly exact copies of some great old instruments, he has evolved more and more, always adding a little extra Zygmuntowicz into the mix. He is unafraid to broaden a shoulder slightly, say, or add some weight to a hip. But the changes remain slight. Sam is always performing his own balancing act between tradition and innovation.

Following his standard procedure, Sam started the Drucker fiddle by building a rib structure around a wooden mold. The ribs are thin strips of wood, barely thicker than veneer. Usually, violin makers use maple for the ribs, often matching the maple that will be used for the back. The ribs are the connector between belly and back. If you lay a violin down on a table and think of it as a house, the back forms the floor, the belly is the roof, and the ribs are the walls—in this case undulating walls bent into shape by heating the thin wood, much as boat builders steam boards to make them bend into shape for the curved hull.

Sam keeps a number of molds in the shop, some based on Stradivari instruments, some on Guarneri, and some of his own devising, though a casual observer could never tell the differences among them. The molds are the practical engineering behind the magical box, and they look the part. If the finished fiddle will look like a shapely woman, the molds more resemble manikins. Usually, the blocks are drilled through with a number of half-dollar-size holes, which allow clamps to be inserted to help hold the newly curved ribs to their shapes. The holes make the forms look like an outsize fiddle-shaped Swiss cheese.

To choose which shape he would follow for the Drucker violin, Sam was forced to make an intuitive leap of faith. After their early discussions about simply making a modern copy of the Rosgonyl Strad, Gene's input could only be musical, not technical.

"Gene hasn't given me a lot of guidance," Sam said. "He just showed me what he does and the instrument he has now and what he doesn't like about it and what he does. I let him play a couple of fiddles I had here in the shop and I could see what he was gravitating toward." That was the sound of a Guarneri del Gesù.

Giuseppe Guarneri was born in Cremona in 1698, and became the third generation of a violin-making family that included his grandfather Andrea (a somewhat older contemporary and lesser-known rival of the young Stradivari), and his father, who through some twist of fate became known mainly in relation to *his* father and signed his instruments "Giuseppe, son of Andrea." Though he didn't really need to, in order to separate his work from *his* father's, young Joseph began labeling his instruments with a cross and the letters *IHS*, and thus became known as "del Gesù."

As a craftsman, Antonio Stradivari was the Laurence Olivier of luthiers, a technically skilled and disciplined workman who labored nobly through a long life, a professional whose normal working level was higher than most, and who regularly scaled peaks of genius. Guarneri was the James Dean of the craft. The Hill brothers also wrote a book on the Guarneri family. In the chapter on Giuseppe del Gesù they repeat the unproved theory that he may have been killed at the age of forty-six. There is some evidence that he quit making violins for a time to run a tavern. One theory claims that some of his fiddles were produced while he was serving a stint in jail. One thing is certain: the man had talent. Despite the turmoil of his personal life, the Hills concluded that Guarneri del Gesù "gave to the world, during fifteen to twenty brief years, violins ... which will ever be acclaimed by the lover of our subject as instruments of unsurpassable charm and originality."

In broad strokes, the great instruments made by Guarneri—there are just dozens left today—are considered more powerful and darker sounding than Strads. The great solo violinists covet Guarneris for that reason. Over the years, Sam Zygmuntowicz designed a violin model that closely approximated a well-known Guarneri known as the Plowden. "It's from 1735, and it's my favorite," Sam says. "It's just right when he was at the peak of his craftsmanship and knowledge."

When Zygmuntowicz worked at René Morel's restoration shop, the actual Plowden would arrive for repairs. "I didn't even know who owned it," Sam remembers.

"I used to put it on my desk during lunch break and just look at it, like a book—just stare at it while I was eating my sandwich. And I would sort of surreptitiously take measurements and set up quick kamikaze photo sessions. So I got some basic information on it and I designed my Guarneri model from there."

Because the model morphed into something of his own, Sam, as a little inside joke, grafted the first letter of his name onto the title and began calling his model the Zowden. For Gene Drucker's instrument, Sam would alter the Zowden shape a little by introducing some of the characteristics of a 1742 Guarneri that was once owned and played by Jascha Heifetz, the David. (Heifetz's will left it to a museum in San Francisco.)

It is yet another example of the tangled knot of tradition and whimsy in the violin world that gives the well-known, collector-quality Cremonese violins their names. For instance, the Plowden is named for a collector and amateur violinist, Lord Plowden, who owned the fiddle almost two hundred years ago. Sometimes, a famous violinist becomes inextricably linked with an instrument and it comes to be named for him, like the Kreisler. But that did not happen with the great Paganini's favorite fiddle, an instrument that was so powerful that it was descriptively nicknamed the Cannon and is still called that. Perhaps the most legendary violin Stradivari ever made was one that was still in his workshop when he died and, according to one legend, had been played only once by the master himself. It is called the Messiah. It still is never played but sits in a glass case in the Ashmolean Museum at Oxford University, a gift from the Hills of London, the family of dealers whose three siblings wrote the famous book on Stradivari.

Sam Zygmuntowicz was able to get his hands on and study a fair number of the greatest violins during his time with René Morel and Jacques Français. The shop, on the eleventh floor of a nondescript building on 54th Street in Manhattan, is a sort of Lourdes for great string players traveling through New York. At any given time millions of dollars worth of Cremonese fiddles are in for repair and healing. Morel, who often schedules his time in fifteen-minute segments, spends much of each day adjusting violins for a continuous stream of glamorous soloists and workaday orchestral fiddlers, who feel their instrument is out of sorts.

Sam speaks often of his apprentice years at the shop, sometimes describing it as a sort of postgraduate training, other times making it seem like a sentence at a prison work farm. In the days I spent with him at the violin-making workshop in Ohio, Sam several times made good-natured jokes that he and many of his peers were ex-hippies in various stages of reconstruction—men (and a few women) of a certain age who'd been drawn to the trade by a 1970s-vintage desire to avoid corporate life, get closer to nature, and learn a craft. Sure enough, quite a few of the other violin makers I met in Oberlin lived in small rural towns and gave off a faint whiff of patchouli.

René Morel was no hippie looking for an alternative lifestyle. He'd been trained in Mirecourt to execute the various techniques of violin making—the many cuts—

with skill and efficiency. Morel often told the story of arriving as a young man at the great Manhattan restoration shop of the day, the House of Wurlitzer, and amazing everyone with the speed and accuracy of his carving.

"Guys like René were just expected to turn out fiddles," Sam said. "It was all handwork and they were trained to be very good technically, very fast, consistent and uniform. It wasn't all that inspiring-looking work, but each of those guys was expected to do a minimum of two violins a week, and the fast guys did three.

"I never have practiced that particular brand of production. I don't think I could do it. You don't waste any unnecessary action. You don't reflect on anything. It's kind of the opposite of my personal process, which includes a lot of patient reflection. But the actual techniques of people like René Morel and Carl Becker—these old guys really know how to get it done."

Carl Becker is a Chicago-based violin maker, now in his nineties, and one of the most respected in the country. Sam stopped to visit Becker when he was on a cross-country tour as a teenager and showed the master a fiddle on which he'd done a complicated restoration. "He was the first real violin maker I'd ever met, and he was nice enough to talk to me," Sam remembers. "He just looked at my violin and said, 'Well, it's not as bad as it could be.'" After Sam finished his first year at the violin school in Salt Lake City, he was offered a job in Becker's shop. Sam went to work with Becker for a summer, when, following his own tradition, Becker moved out to a Wisconsin farm and focused on making violins.

"It was a really intense experience for me," Sam remembers. "In Wisconsin it was total immersion and human contact deprivation, except for the Becker family. I lived in a cabin in the woods without water or plumbing. Washed in a lake. Carried my water from the next piece of property.

"It was great. Carl was a great teacher—a very clear, analytical mind. Quite a bit of what I still do is based on what I learned there." Sam thought about leaving school and staying with Becker. "But," he says, "it's a family business, and I knew I would never be a Becker." He returned to Salt Lake City to finish his degree. Though he is careful not to say anything bad about the school's director, Peter Paul Prier, he makes it clear that they were not always on good terms. "It was kind of frustrating," he says of his time in Salt Lake. "I never had anyone really engage me in a challenging way." Another Salt Lake student remembers that on graduation day, Sam stood up and sang the song "My Way."

It was through the influence of Carl Becker and then René Morel that Zygmuntowicz became firmly convinced that before he could become himself, he would have to learn the skills required to uphold the tradition of his craft.

One day, while we sat in his shop, Sam recalled something Carl Becker had told him during that summer more than twenty years ago, and he suddenly veered off the specific subject—which was the arching of a violin belly—and said, "There's a great essay by T. S. Eliot called 'Tradition and the Individual Talent.' I think that's a great essay. One of his points is that if you're really an incredibly original thinker then it's great that you make up totally new things. But the tradition is a guarantee that the average person doing average things is going to work at a good level. A certain level of knowledge has been accumulated, and the difference between us and our predecessors is that we have more to draw upon. And part of what we draw upon is them. Their experience is now part of our knowledge base."

The Hill brothers espoused this idea many years before Sam Zygmuntowicz—or Eliot for that matter. Stradivari, they wrote, "was in touch with the outcome of well-thought-out experiments, and the traditions which had been evolved and transmitted by the different makers during this long period.... Each generation added its link to the chain, and Stradivari finally welded the whole together."

In the many hours I would spend with Sam watching him work, there was plenty of time where the only sound in the room was the relentless raspy scratch as he scraped at tone wood with one of his tools. But this was one of the times when he was building a head of steam to talk.

"There's a beauty to traditional systems like violin making," he said. "If you just take a beautiful fiddle as a model and try to make one like that, you will hit most of the important points—automatically. You don't really need to understand it, if you stay within the established system.

"To some extent that's the way it was done by the old guys. Since they had been such a part of an ongoing tradition and had been working for a number of generations in a similar style and living in the same area where there was direct transmission from one craftsman to another, it was a reasonable assumption that the accumulated experience was onto something.

"You could safely say that the violin has been resistant to innovation," he said. "There's a funny chapter in Heron-Allen's book that I think is called 'The Violin, Its Variants and Vulgarities.' It lists all kinds of things, like a porcelain violin and a fiddle with a gramophone horn coming out of it, a trapezoid violin—things like that.

"People often ask the question of why the violin hasn't changed in hundreds of years. The implication is that it would somehow be better and more natural if it did. *But why?* If you look at natural forms they're quite resistant to change. Most mutations die out. People often ask why there haven't been improvements in violins. Well there have, but most people don't know enough to understand. There have been huge changes, but the basic chassis looks the same." He had stopped working on his fiddle. It turned out he was just getting started. "This brings me to a tirade," he warned.

"If I may be so obnoxious as to say so—violin making is a kind of un-American activity. It goes against one of our fundamental beliefs, which is that things always get better and the new replaces the old—*Progress.*

"There is really no good answer to why people still play music from three hundred years ago. But to the people who do it and who like listening to it—they would ask, 'Why would you play anything else?'

"The other thing is that violin making has been immune to mechanization and standardization. There have always been a lot of articles that start something like this: 'For three hundred years the secret of Stradivari had eluded violin makers. Now professor so and so at the university of so and so may have found the answer....'

"The reason this is appealing as a story is that it's the American way. There must be a trick. It's like the secret of vulcanizing rubber is to add sulfur to the rubber and, Eureka! And the guy who patented the process became a millionaire. An enterprising guy without the wool pulled over his eyes sees to the heart of the matter and finds the trick, patents it, and cashes out.

"It's a very foreign idea that violin making is not all that mysterious, but it is one of those things where the basic way it works best was stumbled onto a long time ago. The requirements haven't changed, and therefore the results haven't changed and therefore it's a very complex custom that is only learned through long application and a great deal of knowledge. It's not arcane knowledge; it's something any guy can learn—*if you spend thirty years doing it.*

"At the heart of all those articles is the idea that someone is going to figure out the secret and then they'll be able to make millions of violins that are affordable, instead of those really expensive violins that people pay lots of money for and—the implication is—are not really worth it. Once they find the trick they'll be able to mass-produce them. That's the unspoken thought behind that." Then, Sam picked up his knife, started cutting the fiddle again, and was quiet for a long while.

It seems that almost every aspect of violin *making* has its parallel in violin *playing*. Though there are always new prodigies popping up, no one who loves classical music would argue too strongly against the idea that, as Sam said about his craft, "the basic way it works best was stumbled onto a long time ago."

Gene Drucker had the advantage of growing up in a musical household and essentially followed his father into the same trade—a tradition that was quite common among the great violin makers. But Drucker will tell you that his strongest musical influence was not his father, but his private study with Oscar Shumsky. Shumsky was the last student of Leopold Aüer, a Hungarian born in the mid–nineteenth century, who had a brilliant musical career in czarist Russia. Tchaikovsky wrote his only violin concerto for Aüer and planned to dedicate it to him. In 1918, after the Bolshevik revolution, the violinist came to America and for the rest of his life primarily devoted himself to teaching. Before Shumsky, Aüer had taught Efrem Zimbalist and Jascha Heifetz.

In his own treatise on the subject, *Violin Playing as I Teach It*, published in 1921, Aüer attacked the notion of upholding traditions of performance practice, like copying an exact vibrato, or slavishly following a bowing technique. He thought it sucked the life out of new talent. Yet he was a living link in a great chain. One of his teachers was Joseph Joachim, another Hungarian who studied in Vienna, played for a time in Leipzig, and landed in Berlin. While Joachim lived in Vienna, according to the violin encyclopedist Alberto Bachman, he turned the Austrian city into "the Mecca for all violinists." Bachman traces Joachim's artistic family tree back to Joseph Böhm, from Böhm back to Pierre Rode (who has a famous Stradivari named for him), and from Rode back to Giovanni Battista Viotti, who is widely acknowledged to have invented violin playing as it has come down to us. "It is not too much to say," Bachman writes, "that whenever we may have occasion to admire some violinist at the present time, we can go back to Viotti in order to discover the origin of his art."

So, from Gene Drucker to Giovanni Battista Viotti, two violinists born on different continents two hundred years apart, we essentially have only six degrees of separation. It's impossible to quantify the influences, but there is a golden braid connecting the men who keep the tradition with those who invented it. This legacy is not willed like an antique breakfront. If you read T. S. Eliot on the subject, you would learn that Tradition "cannot be inherited, and if you want it you must obtain it by great labour." Gene Drucker, in his understated self-estimation, says, "I was always a practicer." Of the influence of Oscar Shumsky, Drucker says, "It would be impossible not to model one's approach to violin playing and music in general after such a strong example." When he hears some recordings from his early career, Drucker thinks, "I sound like the poor man's Shumsky."

There is another line in Eliot's essay that seems to apply more directly to violin makers. The artist, he wrote, "must be quite aware of the obvious fact that art never improves, but that the material of art is never quite the same."

One day in 1987, Sam Zygmuntowicz took on the challenge of taking new material and trying to duplicate the unimprovable. It was a major moment in his career.

When Sam first struck out on his own, after his apprenticeship with Morel, he initially gained notice in the violin world for his ability to copy old instruments. Stewart Pollens, a violin historian who curates the stringed instrument department of the Metropolitan Museum of Art, had seen a couple of Sam's copies at violin conferences. He convinced the most prestigious journal of the string instrument world, *The Strad*, to commission Zygmuntowicz to copy a Guarneri del Gesù fiddle built in 1733, the one that had come to be known as the Kreisler. Pollens documented the process for the magazine.

In a way, copying a great fiddle is like studying with the master himself. "It's a little bit like taking coaching from someone—very detailed coaching," Sam says. "Not from a person, but from the instrument that person created. Studying a violin from the outside is like learning French in high school. *Making* a copy is like going to France and living there for a couple years."

For this project, Sam only needed to travel to Washington, D.C., where the Kreisler is kept at the Library of Congress's Music Division. There, he performed two parallel feats of learning. The first was to take the violin and, as he says, "turn it into information."

The features most of us notice about a violin are gross characteristics, the kind of things we might use to describe a suspect to a police sketch artist—high forehead, brown eyes, weak chin. In fiddle terms the features a layman would be able to describe are the color of the varnish, the width and curves of the shoulders and hips, the depth of the "waist," which is technically known as the C bout. With a little training and experience, an observer might be able to pick out the way the tricolor outline of purfling is laid into the circumference of the instrument, and maybe the flare of the corners or the distinctive wood carving on the nautilus-shaped scroll on top of the neck.

But to Sam Zygmuntowicz that level of observation is like discerning that the leaves of a tree are green. Using precise rulers and calipers, he measured the Kreisler to tenths of a millimeter. Years before, when the instrument was taken apart for repair in Morel's shop, he'd gotten measurements of the graduated thicknesses of belly and back. He had a chart that analyzed the varying thicknesses of the belly in such detail that it resembled a topographical map. In the Library of Congress, he traced all the outlines and the shape and placement of the distinctive f-shaped holes that are cut into the violin's belly on either side of the bridge. He took photographs in different kinds of light, trying to understand the real nature of the varnish. He even played the fiddle himself to get a sense of its sound.

Sam later wrote his own article on the copying process for *The Strad*. "To a luthier," he wrote, "copying is a window back to a golden age. Makers often study the minutiae of these instruments with a zeal that borders on fanaticism, and with a reverence that is almost religious.

The process of copying lies somewhere between detective work and a spiritual quest. You try to push away the veil of time and see not only the finished product, but how the old makers achieved their results."

Years later, he would talk about copying Guarneri to a gathering of the Violin Society of America. "Making a copy of an old instrument seems like a clear-cut objective," Sam told his colleagues. "It is a technical challenge, but conceptually it shouldn't be so bad: measure the original, find some matching hunks of wood, and carve away anything that doesn't look like a Guarneri."

Even then, his goal was to make more and more instruments that looked and sounded like a Zygmuntowicz. Not only did his prowess as a copyist give him insight into the minute techniques of the masters, it also advanced his reputation—as a copyist. A cover story in *The Strad* was a piece of advertising that no violin maker could buy. The magazine quoted Jacques Français calling Sam's finished Kreisler copy "probably the finest copy of a Guarneri I have ever seen." Another violinist who dealt with Français ordered his own copy of the Kreisler from Sam. Not long after that, Sam got that call from Isaac Stern. The Stern commissions only added to Sam's reputation in the wider world (he ended up on what was then called Public Television's *MacNeil-Lehrer NewsHour*) and in the more hermetic society of string players. With this success, though, came the danger that he would be not freed by the tradition, but hobbled. Violin makers can charge more for faithful "antiqued" copies than they can for modern instruments that actually look new. It could have been a lucrative course to make copies all his life.

By the end of his speech to the Violin Society of America, Sam promised that he would soon give up making copies. "Copies are a kind of sport," he said, "but if you see a lot of Guarneri copies together it is like watching a convention of Elvis impersonators."

Sam then pushed increasingly to convince violinists that he could build them a fiddle that looked quite similar to the old masters, but what he really hoped to do was create a new sound they were looking for, conceiving the fiddle not so much as a re-creation of a museum piece, but as a living, working machine for making music. The higher the level of the client, the more important it became to make not a copy, but a Zygmuntowicz.

"It is almost unfortunate that through putting too much stress on each project I have transformed what would normally be a more relaxed craft into a higher stress one," Sam told me. "It doesn't have to be that way. I could just make one violin after another in my style and I think I would do all right—someone would buy them.

"Many of the projects have a little story in my mind—who it's going to, how it's going to work, *if* it's going to work."

Gene Drucker became a kind of test case for this new process.

It remains the constant, enduring paradox of violin making. No matter how much modern makers learn of the traditions, no matter how much scientific analysis they apply to the materials and techniques, no matter how careful their measurements and analysis of the old instruments, they are still confronted by fiddle players yearning for something that is incredibly hard to describe: a sound.

"Different violinists are known for very distinctive types of playing and sound," Sam Zygmuntowicz says. "Of course, a musician almost never knows enough about it technically to come to me and tell me how to achieve that sound."

Gene Drucker, though an exceptionally articulate man, was no exception. As he had told me, "There's a problem when it comes down to describing sound. The words we have available to us simply don't work very well."

It was time for me to enter the unnameable realm of sound.

Chapter 7

BACH AND THE
PROBLEM WITH
WORDS

*A*fter our vegetarian lunch, on that fine
sunny day when I met Gene Drucker,
we walked back to his apartment
building. In the cool stone-lined lobby four somewhat
nervous-looking young people waited with instrument
cases. It was a student string quartet from a college in upstate New York, and Gene had promised to give them a
coaching session. "You're welcome to sit and watch," he
told me. "If you think that would be enjoyable." I thought
it would, so we all squeezed into the elevator—six people,
four instruments—and unloaded on the thirteenth floor.

There, Gene unlocked the door to a small one-bedroom unit, a little dark and furnished sparely, with a bit of a ragtag feel. He and his family occupied a larger apartment in the same building, but he'd grabbed this place years ago and kept it as a rehearsal studio. Lately, now that he and his wife had a child, they offered the apartment to a music student who was willing to trade rent for childcare chores.

As the young musicians broke out their instruments and tuned up, Gene chatted with them about his friend, who taught at their college and sent them to the city for this coaching. The group was just a school ensemble; it didn't have a name. The players were working on one of the Beethoven quartets and had brought that to play for Drucker.

Of course, the Beethoven quartets are standards of the string quartet repertory and are constantly performed and frequently recorded. The Emerson often placed them in their programs and had made a recording of the full Beethoven quartet cycle for Deutsche Grammophon. It won a Grammy Award and was called "a spectacular achievement" by one reviewer. Gene Drucker knew this music inside and out.

The students did not. But they were talented players, and for the next hour or so they plowed into the music with a mix of verve and ineptitude that was charming and inspiring. Even bunched into a plain little living room with the dead acoustics of a closet, it was hard for the four string players to not occasionally create beautiful music with the soaring sonorities of the master. Drucker was intense, yet also patient and kind. He only stopped the group a few times to correct some rhythmic interpretations by the cellist, a tall young man with an Eastern European accent and a ready willingness to laugh at himself. This was a fun way to spend a late afternoon. Watching Drucker coach these kids made me think of a phrase from an essay by Oliver Wendell Holmes, father of the famous supreme court justice, about a great old violin: as Holmes said of the fiddle, Gene's pores were filled with music. As the rehearsal ended, the de facto leader of the quartet asked Gene how much they should pay him; he told them to keep their money.

After the students packed up and left, Gene and I got back on the elevator and went up a floor to his real apartment, which was bright and clean and tastefully furnished, with a small grand piano dominating the living room. Gene opened a cabinet and pulled out two compact discs and handed one to me.

It contained the music of Béla Bartók, his favorite modern composer, including the Hungarian composer's solo violin sonata and a collection of violin duets, where Gene teamed with his Emerson colleague Phil Setzer. "That might be interesting to you," he said, a little shyly. "If you like Bartók." I told him I did.

"I always enjoyed playing the solo repertoire," Gene told me. "At one time I had an appetite to try to build an auxiliary career in that direction, but that's really diminished in me over the last ten years. Because of my family. First it was losing my father." The violinist Ernest Drucker had died in 1993 from amyotrophic lateral sclerosis—Lou Gehrig's disease.

"At the time that sort of knocked the wind out of me,"

Gene said. "Looking back on that time I can't believe all the things I was doing in the half year before he died. Constantly running out to Queens to see him in a nursing home. Going there, coming back, doing concerts with the quartet, making two Bartók recordings. I can't even remember what the quartet was recording then, but I remember we did a series of radio recordings in St. Paul.

"Then nine months after my father died my son Julian was born, and that transformed my life. Of course I've been very active with the quartet and have played concertos with orchestras a number of times. But recording is a much different investment of time. You have to decide that you really, really want to do that, and then you have to ask ... well, why?"

He handed me the other CD. Inside the jewel case was a jacket that featured a picture of Gene, wearing a tuxedo and a very serious look, posed playing the fiddle. The photo seemed classic and old-fashioned, as if it had been taken decades ago. His looks are simply from a different era. This recording was Drucker's solo climb up one of the great peaks of the violin repertory, the unaccompanied sonatas and partitas by Johann Sebastian Bach.

"This was reissued recently," he said. "It's gotten some nice reviews, but it hasn't really been a career-building thing for me. It's just really nice to have this record to show what I can do."

I have an old vinyl record on which Pablo Casals talks about music and particularly about J. S. Bach. I haven't listened to it for years—like many people I've let my turntable fall into disrepair—but I vividly remember one thing the cellist says: *Bach is all I dream about in music*. I feel the same way. There are periods in my life where I listen to Bach every day. And it is a near certainty that on those days I practice the trumpet, I will play something by Bach. So I gratefully took this musical offering from Gene Drucker and played it as soon as I got home.

Bach wrote this music in the second decade of the eighteenth century, while he was employed by Prince Leopold of Anhalt-Cöthen. The composer famously said that all of his voluminous musical output was designed for the greater glory of God. But Prince Leopold demanded that his kapellmeister write secular instrumental music, so these six pieces for solo violin are part of the relatively small segment of his work that is strictly secular. They were written fairly early in the history of the modern violin—Stradivari was still making instruments—yet they stretch the technical demands on the performer to a breaking point. Nearly three hundred years have passed and they remain a high technical hurdle and an enduring musical monument.

I did my best to drop out of music school (several different schools, in fact) before I was forced to take the courses in formal musical analysis. Consequently, when I sliced open the plastic wrapping on Drucker's Bach recording, started reading the liner notes, and encountered this— "The first two movements are coupled together in the manner of an improvisatory prelude and extended fugue, the latter continually alternating between strict polyphony and single-line passage work. The third movements release the tension and provide welcome tonal relief, while the finales share the symmetrical plan of a typical binary suite movement."— I was ready to throw the booklet across the room. But lower on that first page I came to a section of analysis written by Drucker himself. In the second paragraph he began, "The quickest route into Bach's mind ..." I closed the liner notes and slipped the booklet back into the CD case. In my view, the quickest way into Bach's mind would be to stop reading and start listening.

The scientist James Q. Wilson once wrote of Bach's Mass in B Minor that it was the sound of the entire world thinking at once. In comparison, the solo violin works seem more the musings of a single solitary genius. And at first they are strange. Most of the violin playing most of us know is the sectional work of an orchestra—fifty or so fiddlers playing single-note lines simultaneously. With all these players working together, the edges get rounded off. The result is that one of the most frequent descriptions of an orchestral string section's sound is *lush*. In contrast, a violinist playing alone can sound surprisingly edgy and intense.

For his solo works, Bach usually allowed the violin to play a single line, but often he exploited the ability of the instrument to play several notes at the same time. This is accomplished by running the bow over two or three strings at once. (Getting the hair of the bow to touch all four strings is impossible on the modern violin and bow, which has led some to speculate that there was a specially curved bow during Bach's day. Centuries later, someone invented a highly curved "Bach bow," but it never caught on.) In the solo sonatas and partitas there are many passages that do present *polyphony*: two or more notes at once, but the bulk of the compositions consists of single-note passages of such supremely logical complexity that there needs to be no other sound.

This was not always obvious. Despite his widely recognized mastery, Bach's work went out of fashion for a time after his death. When it was being rediscovered during the late Classical age, at least two great composers— namely Schumann and Mendelssohn—suspected that there was no way Bach expected a violinist to play this music alone. There must have been keyboard accompaniment that was lost in the mists of time. Each wrote his own version of keyboard support for the violin. They are musical curiosities but largely wasted effort.

To look at this music on the page, one understands the enormous complexity of the compositions. There are masses of notes, page after page of music manuscript just filled top to bottom with black ink. It would seem that among all that music there would be room for a few flubs, an improvisation or two. But I have played bits of the partitas on the trumpet, and one changed note sounds immediately like a crime against nature. And indeed, Gene Drucker would write that this music had the quality of a natural phenomenon, as if it has always existed and always would.

As much as I marveled at Bach's music, and was captivated by Drucker's interpretation, after getting through the pieces once, I knew I really needed to listen at a different level, to tunnel into this great musical edifice and explore the inner recesses, the nooks and crannies of the sound. I would try to use this violin masterpiece to understand better what all the fuss was about with fiddles. Turning the listening experience into interpretation would prove difficult. After all, Drucker himself, that most articulate of men, had warned me that words are often lacking when it comes to describing sound. "It's kind of like that idea that Eskimos have many different words to describe snow," he'd said. "In this case there aren't that many words that really have the right meaning and describe sound accurately. I love words, but they often fail me in this context."

The man who taught Sam Zygmuntowicz violin making in school, Peter Paul Prier, once wrote an article for the *Journal of the Violin Society of America*, in which he listed some essential words that could be employed to describe the sound of a fiddle. Here they are: *hard, mellow, even, nasal, open, ringing, muted, round, full, hollow.*

Prier gave some explanation for each term. For instance, a mellow sound was a sweet, rich, and warm tone. Nasal meant making a kind of *"eeee"* sound, a little pinched. Open was the sound most liked by musicians, Prier said, like the sound of someone saying *"oooh."*

Gene Drucker had some terminology of his own. "When my Strad is at its best it has a very classy, aristocratic sound," he told me. I guess *classy* meant something, though I wondered if a bad-sounding fiddle could be described as "trashy." But what did *aristocratic* sound like? I didn't want to bother Gene, but I started asking myself: does he mean the enlightened aristocracy of Peter the Great of Russia, or the dysfunctional aristocracy of Louis XVI?

Somehow, listening to Drucker play Bach armed with Prier's terms seemed to make the job harder. Yes, at times Gene's Stradivari sounded open; at other times full and sometimes ringing. Yet there were plenty of moments when Gene's fiddle sounded muted or mellow, maybe even a touch nasal now and then. I began listening to sections of the three sonatas and three partitas every day, often with very expensive headphones for sonic intimacy, just as often letting the music roar loudly through the speakers. My fiancée, Jana, began to complain. She has wide, eclectic musical tastes and we rarely argue about what gets played in the house. Classical music is not really her thing, but she had been enthusiastic about attending Emerson Quartet concerts. She drew the line at Bach's music for solo violin. "That music makes me nervous," she said. I promised to always don the headphones when she was home.

Despite all the close listening I was doing, I wasn't making much headway into the mysteries of sound and kept searching for clues in the *Journal of the Violin Society*. I came across an article by Norman Pickering, an acoustics expert whom Sam mentioned often in our time together, always with admiration. Pickering has done as much scientific analysis of violin tone as anyone. He compiled his own list of words for sound and it was quite a bit longer than Prier's.

"*Rough, hollow, thin, pure, flutey, metallic, resonant, dry,*" Pickering began, and went on for a long paragraph. "*Somber, clear, even, uneven, brilliant, wolfy, elegant, lively, raw, sonorous, muted, dark, light, plumy, tubby, harsh, pinched, aggressive, silky, silvery, golden, noble, constricted, smooth, mellow, bright, dull, piercing, shrill, nasal, fuzzy, scratchy, rich, full, weak, powerful, sweet.*"

That sure was a lot of words! Certainly, armed with that extensive nomenclature, I could analyze the sound of Drucker's Strad. But, Pickering warned, to someone with a scientific view these words are red flags. They might be comprehensive, but hardly precise.

Scientists have been studying the sound of the violin for about as long as the violin has been around, and you could easily get into an argument with any violin maker on whether it's done any good. There is evidence that Galileo studied the properties of the pitches of plucked strings in the mid–1600s.[5] But it wasn't until the 1880s that a German scientist named H. L. F. Helmholtz figured out how to accurately measure the vibrations that create sound and became a pioneer in the science of acoustics.

Just as often, it is not only the required courses in technical musical analysis, but also the required course in acoustics that make music students like me decide to drop out. The field is full of sine waves and amplitudes and cycles and frequencies, but all the layman really needs to

---

[5] Around that same time Galileo ordered through a priest a Cremonese violin for his nephew. There is a funny series of letters from the cleric to the scientist explaining with mounting apologies why it is taking so long to get the fiddle and how come the price keeps going up. The more things change …

understand is something called the harmonic series. Basically, no musical tone is pure. If it were, listening to it would be torture. Instead, if you walk up to a piano and play a middle C, that tone would be prominent, but also sounding is a C one octave above that, and a G above that, and another C above that, and an E above that, and another G still higher, and more and more tones, all in a fixed mathematical relationship. It is the relative strength of the various tones in this harmonic series—think of them as ghost notes—that contributes fundamentally to the quality of sound. Some instruments—like flutes—don't produce a very rich and full overtone series. What gives the bowed string instruments their character is that they all produce a full overtone series. But not all overtone series are created equal, and that's what separates the great instruments from the lesser.

By now, many great fiddles have been acoustically analyzed and measured. The scientists know, for instance, that a certain great Stradivari has stronger frequencies in some areas of its sound spectrum than in others. But there is no way to translate that into a set of rules for someone like Sam Zygmuntowicz to follow in building a new instrument. And usually, even very smart people like Gene Drucker do not speak the language of acoustics. He could not go into Sam's workshop and write a bunch of equations on a blackboard. The fiddler and the luthier are stuck with using words, vague and nebulous words.

And so, as is true with so many other facets of the fiddle, when it comes to analyzing sound, sentiment often trumps science.

For instance, Jacques Français, the famous dealer descended from generations of luthiers, said that his father always told him that a violin began to sound like its owner, and the longer it was played by one person, the longer it would take to change sounds when acquired by a new owner. There was a strong school of thought that says the fiddler makes the fiddle. In the late 1970s, Alexander Schneider of the Budapest String Quartet left his del Gesù in a taxi and it looked like it would be lost forever. When his friend the flutist and journalist Eugenia Zukerman (then wife of violinist Pinchas) called Schneider to commiserate over his loss, he told her he had mourned for a while, but then realized: "You play as you are, and what you are as a human being will come through no matter what you play on."[6] This view is supported by Sir James Beament, the Cambridge don who wrote the wonderful *Violin Explained*. In listening experiments he'd done, Beament reported, people could often recognize, sight unseen, a *player*, but almost never an *instrument*.

Then there is the question of what I was really hearing when I tried to analyze Drucker's sound. I remembered Gene's common phrase—what you hear under your ear. Since I don't play the fiddle, I could not experience that particular sensation. I was listening to the Bach on a recording, and more often than not with headphones, so I was getting more intimate contact with the sound than someone sitting in a concert hall. In fact, Gene told me

---

[6.] Schneider's violin was returned months later by some rock musicians who'd taken the same taxi later that day. When asked how he felt being reunited with his fiddle, the violinist didn't bother trying to use words; he picked up the del Gesù and played Bach.

later, the Bach was recorded in two sessions with two different producers, two different technologies (analog first, then digital), and two locations that were quite different acoustically—a resonant church and a dry college recital hall. All sorts of technical work was required in the final mixing of the music to make it sound consistent and "natural." So, I might know how a recording engineer could simulate the sound of five rows back from the stage, but I would never really know what the violin sounded like in Drucker's left ear, and that was really the most important place, since that spot was the locus of the complicated feedback loop that gives each player his or her particular sound. It is at this point that connection between violinist and violin begins to be not just intimate, but downright symbiotic. Pinchas Zukerman once described it this way: "You feel the vibrations going through your head, deep into your throat. At very intense moments I actually choke when I play. But there are also moments of intense physical pleasure."

Out of the thirty-two sections that make up Bach's works for solo violin, the most famous is the final movement of the Partita no. 2 in D minor—the Chaconne. There is a whole literature devoted to that section alone, fifteen or so minutes of music that plenty of people think is among the most glorious ever written. Based on a relatively simple theme, the piece provoked one of Bach's biographers, Spitta, to write that the Chaconne was a triumph of spirit over substance. That might seem like something of an insult, unless you read Yehudi Menuhin's autobiography. There, the violinist recounts his early fascination with the Chaconne (he was a prodigy in all aspects) and his youthful belief that if he could play the Chaconne—and play it well enough—in the Sistine Chapel, he might just be able to bring about peace on earth.

Nobody knows the exact circumstances of how Bach wrote any of the unaccompanied partitas for violin. But there is one event from that period in the composer's life that opens up vast spaces for speculation and poignancy.

Bach was in his early thirties when he was working in Axhalt-Cöthen, married and already the father of several children (he'd eventually father twenty). His patron, Prince Leopold, was an avid traveler, and he often convinced his kappelmeister to accompany him. When Bach returned from one such trip in 1720, he found that his wife, Maria Barbara, had died in his absence. Could his mourning explain why these pieces are so counterintuitive, why there is such majesty in music designed for one lonely fiddler?

Over the months I was listening to Drucker playing Bach, I began to gravitate more and more to the Chaconne. I bought the book of sheet music that contained the piece and followed along, often amazed that anyone could actually navigate the technical demands. Even listening with the advantage of someone trained in music, I marveled that Gene could simply play all the notes. It's true that I am a mediocre musician, but I know enough about performing to understand that getting through all those notes *and* turning them into music was like the difference between drafting and animation.

I usually listened late at night (after my fiancée was safely asleep), lying on the carpet in front of the stereo, high-tech headphones clamped on my ears. There were technical aspects of Gene's performance on the violin that I would probably never understand: the complicated choreography of bowing, fingering, vibrato, and things like that. There were aspects of his sound that I might never be able to adequately describe, even armed with an arsenal of words from Peter Paul Prier and Norman Pickering. Yes, it was full and ringing and round and brilliant and smooth and noble. It was even classy and aristocratic, whatever that meant. In the end, it was the *effect* of the sound, not its components, that became so important to me.

Listening to Bach a lot is a pretty sublime way to spend your time. One day in the midst of all this profound sublimity I got a call that yanked me rudely back to harsh reality. My uncle had suddenly become unable to speak, and during emergency brain surgery to remove a tumor his gall bladder had burst, leaving him unconscious, in septic shock, and being kept alive on a respirator in an intensive care unit.

His name was Santino and he'd been a lifelong bachelor. Besides his sister and two brothers, I was his closest relative. His older brother, my father, had recently been diagnosed with lymphoma and was too compromised by chemotherapy to even dare enter the hospital. His older sister, my aunt, couldn't deal with her brother's impending death. After a week of increasingly awful heroic medical procedures, all futile, it was obvious that he would not pull through. So it fell to my other uncle and me to decide finally to let Santino die. And, as things worked out, it fell to me alone to give the final order and to witness his death.

I drove to the hospital in Scranton on a warm June day, a day not unlike the day of the funeral of former Governor Casey, where I'd heard that young violinist play the Irving Berlin song and begun this trip into the world of fiddles. During the drive I listened to Drucker play the Bach Sonata in G and the Partita no. 1, but my thoughts were almost everywhere but the music. I pulled into the hospital garage, parked in a dark corner space, and kept the CD playing. Gene was into the Partita no. 2 and the Chaconne was coming up and I figured another fifteen minutes wouldn't make much difference right then.

There are moments in Drucker's recording when you can hear the violinist breathe, and listening to it then it seemed like the true breath of life. This great edifice of sound that Bach had created was a monument to the spirit of mankind. I'm stealing a phrase from someone, though I can't remember whom: this music was an echo of the human soul itself.

I believe we absolutely need music in our lives—sometimes only music will do. I was too preoccupied that day, but later I realized how lucky I was at this moment to have one of the immortal works of music, performed on an instrument created by the greatest craftsman of all time, played by one of the brightest performers of his generation. If you think that maybe any music would have been solace right then I can assure you that's not true. A few moments later, as I sat in the intensive care unit, watching a nurse gently and competently unhook all the machines that kept Santino alive, a kindly volunteer walked in with a Celtic harp and asked if I'd like her to play. I didn't want to be rude. I said sure and asked if she knew any Bach. She didn't but played "Amazing Grace." When she finished I asked her to please leave.

I might never know the right words to use to describe the great sound of the Stradivari, or to analyze the genius of Bach, but I knew now in some fundamental way what Gene meant when he talked about the "soul nourishment" that playing immortal music on that fiddle had given him. The whole was greater than the sum of the parts, but the parts were essential.

Not long after that I opened again those liner notes Gene had prepared. Of the Chaconne he'd written: "To say that it expresses all the joys and sorrows of this life, as well as a yearning for something beyond life, is no great exaggeration."

When next I returned to Sam's studio, there seemed to be much more at stake.

Chapter 8

CARING MORE
AND MORE
ABOUT LESS
AND LESS

*Violin making is one of the most noble crafts of
man, being one in which the mental and artistic
genius of the maker find full freedom. A man's
true character and nature will be revealed by the violin that he
fashions. If he is a true artist he will build his very soul into
the instrument.*

I came upon that passage during my very first day looking into violin books at the New York Public Library. It
is from a book called *You Can Make a Stradivarius Violin*,
which was written around 1950 by a man named Joseph

V. Reid. Reid was born in Canada and ended up in Illinois, working as an engineer for the American Can Company, and in his spare time trying to make Stradivarius violins. His book is much less eccentric than Edward Heron-Allen's, but no less charming in its earnest postwar can-do attitude.

After reading Reid's book there was a period where I day-dreamed that I might try to build a Stradivarius violin myself. Reid made the whole undertaking seem practical and manageable, like building a coffee table in the basement, or putting together a ham radio from a kit. But I realized that the level of my woodworking skills was just high enough to, say, build a new deck on the back of a little house I own in the Catskills. In the early fall I started doing that in between visits to Sam Zygmuntowicz's workshop in the city.

The fall became glorious that year, and Sam had cleared the odds and ends from his workbench and was ready to work on the Drucker fiddle in earnest, hoping to make a delivery date in the new year—May 17, to be exact, which would be Gene's fiftieth birthday. We started to develop a routine. Sam would call me in the afternoon, usually, and say, "You should come over tomorrow, there's something you might want to see." Since I learned early on that Sam rarely arrived at work before 10 A.M., if the weather was fair, I would leave my apartment in the early morning and walk down into Chinatown, up and over the Brooklyn Bridge, and toward his studio on the far edge of downtown Brooklyn. I now had a set of keys, so I could let myself through the courtyard gate and into the old factory building. His studio door was never locked.

One day I pushed through that heavy metal door, crossed the large room with its worn rugs and furniture and grand piano, and entered the workshop to find Sam with the guts of Gene's violin. To start, he'd performed a series of transfers of the model outline he'd decided to use—his adaptation of the Plowden Guarneri that he called the Zowden.

"I had worked on the real Plowden in René's shop," Sam told me. "That's the fiddle that I would put on my desk during my lunch break and just stare at while I was eating my sandwich. So I got some basic info on it and designed my standard model from there.

"Later the owner called me and asked if I'd like to make a *real* copy of it. I made casts with silicone and exhaustive measurements. But the model we finally renamed the Zowden was one I'd fixed up a little bit. There's a certain amount of slippage between the signified and the signifier, or whatever you would say. You see the real thing and you trace it and you take it home and draw it and it's always different. For instance, I tried to regularize and fix what I thought were bumps and lumps in the original, and I think I made it symmetrical from side to side, where the original is asymmetrical.

"With any of these things there's a weird relationship with the real thing. Distance always creeps in. When people talk about personal style a lot of what they're talking about is slipping away from the original—people were trying to do it just like the original but they didn't. But that's a digression."

However near or far his version strayed from Guarneri's famous fiddle, to start building it, Sam had traced the shape onto a thin sheet of aluminum, and cut that. The aluminum template was then used to carefully cut another outline onto a thick wood block. That shaped wooden piece was the mold, a kind of chassis on which the actual violin would be built.

Now, Sam held up the chassis for me to look at it. In strategic locations on the characteristic feminine shape were small wood blocks, about the size of blocks with which a child might play. Imagining the body to be that of a woman, one block was where the neck joined the torso, two were on either side of where the torso met the waist, two were lower down, on either side of where the hips met the waist, and one last block was at the very center of the bottom, where, on the fiddle, a tailpiece would be attached to help hold the strings tense. "Stradivari often used willow for the blocks," Sam told me. "For Gene's fiddle I used spruce. Anything that's lightweight and strong works fine."

These blocks would never be seen again, once the fiddle was put together. "The blocks are pretty much purely mechanical," Sam told me. "You have to have a good surface to glue the ribs. But there's some aesthetic component. Once it's done, it's the basis for the outline of the instrument. I've made the curves in the blocks a little flatter, so altogether it's a little less voluptuous, a little more of a solid, stocky profile. But not by a lot."

Every day I spent with Sam I understood a little better that on the path a luthier treads leaps are unheard of; each step is a small one.

"There are not many gross variations on the design of a

violin," he continued, "but there are quite some number of minor variations that can be recognized by someone who really knows violins. Someone like Jacques Français, people who make their living dealing fiddles, can tell a Strad from any other fiddle and can tell you roughly what year it was made in. They can look at other violins and tell you what city it came from, maybe who the maker was and when it was made and be accurate to within a few years, more or less. For them it's like a normal person's ability to look into a crowd of faces and pick out someone they know, without looking at every face and saying, 'Is that him, is *that* him?'"

This basic body of the violin that Sam was holding looked like one of those balsa wood models architects make of buildings, where the roof has been taken off to give a view of the little rooms inside. The walls of the fiddle—the ribs—made of maple planed to a thickness of only one-sixteenth of an inch, were clamped onto those six interior wood blocks.

"There's a whole thing to bending the ribs," Sam said. "You bend them on a hot iron. They're made out of curly maple and they break easily, especially if the iron is not hot enough. If the iron is too hot you can burn them. So you have to have just the right temperature and just the right pressure. It's a skill and knack, and if you do it enough it just happens.

"We're letting the ribs dry now and tomorrow we'll glue them. Then we put linings inside the ribs." The linings are made of thin veneer strips of wood that are glued to the inside of the ribs, running parallel on the top and bottom. The linings provide some extra support for the ribs, but primarily they are there to give more contact surface on which to eventually glue the finished top and back. After the ribs and linings were glued and dried, all of the excess wood of the blocks would be shaved away. About half of each block I saw now would be removed. Once that was done the great majority of structural support of the violin's body would be finished, though the work was far from done.

"The next real decision point," Sam said, "is when you start cutting the outlines of the top and back."

Since that curvaceous shape of the top and back is the most prominent feature of a fiddle, I thought it must also be the most important component of the design. Sam quickly set me straight. The pattern of the violin has become so standardized, he informed me, that some violin makers simply use one pattern for their entire career. "There's nothing really wrong with that," Sam said. "That's the way Strad was usually working—with the same basic mold and then making variations while he worked. It was the same thing with Guarneri.

"Having a lot of models to work with slows down your efficiency. It gives you more things to think about. But I get tired of working on the same thing all the time. Each pattern is maybe a little bit different tonally, and a little bit different aesthetically. I feel it allows me to match what I'm doing to the individual player."

Collectors and dealers may talk about the curves and edges on the face of a fiddle, sometimes in flowery language. Violin aesthetes can spend a lot of energy describing the placement and tilt of the f-holes that are cut into the belly of the fiddle on either side of the bridge, which supports the strings. I had read some of these descriptions in exhibition and sales catalogs and started referring to it as "fiddle porn." Sam liked that term when I told it to him, but he had not been totally immune to such effusiveness. In one article he wrote years ago about the Cessole, a Stradivari built in 1716, he noted that the fiddle had "sleek, animated lines. The corners and edge work are prominent but delicate, the ffs upright and lean.... There is a light and nimble character to the work."

But that was years ago, when he was trying to get his name out and build a reputation. Now, in the workshop, Sam left the showmanship aside and acted like an artisan, someone who was simply cutting wood to build a box. Over his years as a builder, he'd increasingly understood the important factor: the violin is a vibrating box. He'd come to the conclusion that the airspace inside that box was far more important to the actual sound of the instrument than delicate edge work or the carving of the distinctive scroll at the top of the neck, no matter how nimbly it was done.

"There are things that are very important for the function of the sound and you want to get that just right and spend as much time as possible to get it to happen right," Sam told me. "And then there are things having to do with the aesthetics, and some people like it one way and some another, but both are fine. Just cutting wood—that's a walk in the park for me."

Through the upcoming weeks I would watch plenty

of wood being cut, but cut in a way that bore no resemblance to the sawing I was doing on my deck upstate. Using many of those odd and ancient-looking tools lined up on his worktable, Sam started fashioning a fiddle. It was a process that he always liked to describe by adapting an old joke about the art of sculpture: how do you make Michelangelo's *David*? Take a block of marble and carve away everything that doesn't look like David. In his case, Sam told me, "I just take a piece of wood and carve away everything that doesn't look like a violin."

One day I climbed the stairs to Sam's studio and found him working intently on a piece of wood that looked an awful lot like a violin. It was the back for the Drucker fiddle, a beautiful piece of maple—an Exhibition Piece Indeed!—that he'd cut into the outline shape. He'd already done preliminary carving of the arching. Sam had the back clamped onto a cloth-covered work surface, and he was slicing into the wood very close to the edge with what looked like a kitchen knife. It turned out it was a kitchen knife, a small blade with a very sharp point, a kind of paring knife, which he'd modified for this task—purfling.

On the front and back plates of a violin, out near the edges, there is a line that traces the outline about four millimeters inside the actual edge of the wood. From a distance, the purfling looks as if it has been drawn or painted on the fiddle, and on some cheap fiddles it *is* simply painted. In a quality instrument, though, the purfling is actually a sandwich of three incredibly thin strips of wood, inlaid into a tiny groove that has been carved around the curving borders of each of the two plates. Because he likes the way he can work with it, Sam often uses wood from a pear tree. Two pieces are dyed black and a strip of poplar in the middle is left light. The whole effect seems to be decorative, but the three bands of wood serve to stop cracks from running from the edge of the fiddle into the interior part of the plates.

Before I'd arrived, Sam had scribed a guideline for the groove he was cutting with a little edge tool designed just for this job. Now, digging that sharp knife into the scribe lines, he pulled the blade carefully, tracing the mark. It took a surprising amount of force to make the cut. Sam's fingers flexed hard on the knife handle, and there were times when he let out a grunt. The groove would only be three millimeters deep, so there wasn't much room for error. Once he cut the two edge lines, he would dig out the wood with another special tool that looks like something a dentist might use. It is called a purfling picker.

"This whole little assembly—the outline, the purfling groove, and then the channel—all that is what I call edge work," he said, staring intently at his knifepoint. "It's not the most important thing, probably, but it has implications. It's really where the aesthetic finesse of making an instrument is visible. If I was judging a violin at a competition, the edge work is where I can see the technique come together. A lot of other things are more important but are not as readily visible."

Minutes went by and accumulated into hours. Sam carved and gouged. Lots of time passed where he was silent. At one point, when the concave curve of the purfling pieces met and the edges of that three-part wood sandwich had to be joined, Sam tried to explain how Stradivari did this job in a distinctive way, creating a sweeping and elegant little pointed corner that Sam jokingly calls the "bumblebee stingerette." There are reams of fiddle porn devoted to describing this feature. I stared and stared as Sam worked to re-create the stingerette in this fiddle, but I just couldn't see what he was trying to show me.

"Go home tonight and read that article I gave you," he said rather sternly. "There's a section on purfling." Sam sounded exasperated. "It's a minor point," he continued. "You just have to be into it." He tried again to show me what was distinctive about the mitered joint of two sections of those three impossibly small pieces of wood. Try as I might, I still couldn't see what was special about the point.

Finally Sam put down his tools and sat back in his chair. "The angle itself is not the big deal," he said, with a distinct tone of disappointment in his voice. "But it's almost impossible for me to talk about it with any sophistication until you can get hooked into the right way of looking at it. It's not that this one thing is all that important in itself, but if you want to understand it, you have to understand that those kinds of things exist. There are hundreds of small tasks like this that come up in the course of making a fiddle. It's not even like my clients know about these little things either. But they know that I'm a person who knows about it."

I stayed a little longer that day, long enough for Sam to perk up and exclaim, "Okay, we're coming to the exciting conclusion! I'm going to go warm up the glue." He uses traditional rabbit hide glue to stick the purfling into the channel. Rabbit hide glue is used almost exclusively by musical instrument makers because it is quite strong, but the bond can be easily broken when repairs are required.

When the viscous glue started steaming in a little electric cooker, Sam took a syrnge, dipped it into the glue, and carefully pushed a sticky bead into the tiny channel he'd dug. The whole studio smelled a little gamey as I was leaving. Sam walked me to the door. "It's good for you to see one part of this from beginning to end," he said. "Because every part of making a violin is a big thing with a lot of details. A lot of those details you really don't want to know."

I tried to be a good student and went home and read the purfling section in Sam's article on violin making, which was adapted from a talk he'd given at the twenty-fourth annual convention of the Violin Society of America. He'd talked about how Stradivari veered a bit from his scribe line to create the bumblebee stingerette and how Guarneri seemed less fussy in his approach. Sam mentioned that there was now a mechanical tool—a little router machine—to create the purfling groove without the painstaking cutting and gouging. He would no sooner use a powered purfling machine than he would sell his son. "People think there is something esoteric and pure about using hand tools," he said to his colleagues that day. "But they are more useful in some ways because they more naturally give you the result you want."

The result he wanted in this case seemed never far from Sam's mind. Almost every time I visited his shop, he would at some point bring up Gene Drucker and his finicky nature. Sam sometimes seemed to be psyching himself up to the challenge, and other times preparing himself for disappointment. Often, he'd start talking about the Drucker fiddle and end up discussing his life's work.

"It might have been interesting to have worked on Gene's Strad a little more," Sam began one day. "If I had a chance to do that I'd know more about his fiddle and more about Gene. But each fiddle of mine he's tried he's liked.

"I'm just hoping the force will be with me on this one. It's not like it's the first fiddle I've ever made; it's not all that mysterious. And let's assume that Gene is finicky, but he's not crazy. And he's finicky because his fiddle is a little capricious, and that's unsettling for him. It is my hope that what I make for him will be on a good day as good as what he's got and will always be less capricious. That result would have the potential of really helping him a lot. That's kind of asking a lot of the project. A more modest upside is that my fiddle provides him something else to play when his Strad is bothering him, or he can spare his Strad the pain of traveling. That would be a totally acceptable outcome, but just not as satisfying as if he retired his Strad. But let's not get ahead of ourselves here."

Sam was working on the violin top—or "belly"—that day. The spruce had been cut and carved in a close approximation of the final arching. The architecture of the upward sweep of a violin belly from the edges to the center is a vital component for sound production, and its design holds nearly endless possibilities. Once again, what had been decided upon three hundred years ago seems to work best. Consequently, Sam used templates to guide his arching. He had traced the archings of a number of great violins during his years working in René Morel's restoration shop.

"The templates are great," he said, "because that way I'm not trying to make the arching the way I feel that day. I have a guide. Right now I'm on a late Guarneri kick and that's what I'm using for Gene's fiddle. Generally the Guarneri arching is a little flatter than Strad's. My teacher Carl Becker used to say that it looked like someone has stretched out a sheet of rubber over something— it's all taut and smooth and low and drawn out. On some Strads the arching seems more sculpted."

The hand tool Sam used this day was a scraper, a sharpened piece of steel that looked like the head of a spatula with no handle. The thin metal slicing off the wood made a short, raspy report. His motions were quick: three or four scrapes in succession and then a pause. "I'm making decisions the whole time I'm doing this," Sam said. "Okay, do I want to go a little deeper in the channel?" (The channel is a sort of gutter, which swoops down just inside the purfling before rising again as the arching climbs to its maximum height in the center of the plate.) "The channel will affect the flexibility of the whole top, and that will affect how it feels to play and how it sounds.

"At this point in the process there are several variables I can choose. The arching height is one. The depth of the channel and the edge work. Then the thicknesses of the top and back. The placement and the size of the f-holes. And the bass-bar."

I came to think of the Drucker violin as something like the Scarecrow in *The Wizard of Oz*, in that scene in the movie when he's being cleaned up and put back together in preparation for meeting the Wizard. Pieces of the fiddle were scattered about the studio—the top on Sam's desk, the back across the room near Wiltrud's workplace, the rib structure stored in a slot near the stereo—all waiting to come together.

Music played nearly constantly throughout the day in the shop, a soft background noise that was often interrupted by bleating car and truck horns from the streets below. I sensed there was some interpersonal dynamic at work, a benign battle over whose favorite music was played. One day, Sam stopped working for a moment to listen more closely to the soundtrack, which was oddly metered and filled with exotic-sounding string instruments. "Wiltrud always accuses me of listening to hillbilly music," he said, "but what's this? It's hillbilly music that happens to be from Macedonia." Wiltrud said something in German to Dietmar, and they both laughed. Sam looked at me with one of those put-upon stares that Jack Benny used so effectively.

All workplaces have a culture of sorts, and this shop had an easygoing feel. I've worked in a few places where the boss prided himself or herself on letting people come and go as they pleased, and creating camaraderie and fun. But it was still a job. Here in Sam's studio there seemed to be no sense that what was going on was even work. It was as if three people had somehow realized separately that there were all these tools in this one place and you could go there and make violins. Sometimes everyone would have lunch together. Other times they went off on their own. Sam was fairly often interrupted by phone calls. Mostly, talk among the colleagues in the workshop was brief and infrequent. Of course, that may have been because I was there, making Sam talk as he worked.

"The other night I came here and worked by myself," he told me one day. "I had to cut the scroll for a cello we're building. We just needed to get it done. It's the kind of thing that's best done late at night with good lights. So I stayed late and had the music going and everybody was gone and I just wacked it out. It was really very pleasurable. But most of what you've come here to see isn't like that."

As the pieces of finished wood accumulated, I began to get the sense that now there was much more on Sam's mind than cutting and carving, that he was moving into a realm of decision making that would affect the quality of the Drucker fiddle in important and irreversible ways. Sure, a lot of what I was watching seemed to be the work of a kindly wood-carver—a Geppetto—but Sam was obviously more than that. There was also an acoustician and an engineer at work. As he approached finishing the spruce top, his progress got slower and slower. He would often stop scraping, make a measurement with calipers he kept close by, and then refer to a notebook on his desk where he kept detailed information on previous fiddles he'd built.

He opened the book to a fiddle he'd made in 1993. "It was not a very high-profile musician," Sam said. "But it was actually a somewhat interesting fiddle. I recorded wood choice, arch height, exact thicknesses." The thicknesses were written on a sheet of paper with a violin outline drawn on. Rings were drawn within the shape that looked like the swirling gradient lines on a topographical map. In more than two dozen spots were measurements of the final wood thickness down to a tenth of a millimeter.

"If there's anything I can measure," Sam said, "I measure it, on the theory that it will become interesting in later years. I'll make some varnish notes, and some evaluations of the sound, and if I can I'll follow up and see how the sound might have changed over time."

"Does every violin maker do this?" I asked.

"No. Some guys take two measurements and that's it. I think I'm kind of a maniac.

"It's a work technique. Not a particularly efficient one, but we're not judged on high efficiency—which is a very good thing. I wouldn't survive, or I'd certainly have to alter my work style, if I had to be more efficient.

"But it's all part of a process of becoming—I don't know what you call it—I guess a more *subtle* worker. The thing is that you start to care more and more about less and less."

What is the essence of craftsmanship? Often, our romantic notion is that it is unnameable, unquantifiable—that certain *je ne sais quoi*. But perhaps the opposite is true, that the beating heart of excellence longs to measure and quantify, to continually care more and more about less and less. James Beament, in his great book on the violin, concluded that Stradivari was a genius, but not the kind of wildman, wunderkind genius that people love to imagine. Guarneri better fit that mold. Strad was a genius of maturity and continuity. He took great pains in his work, and continued to take great pains for a very long time.

Was I watching someone similar in this former factory in Brooklyn? As more and more became less and less, I'd seen a concomitant shrinking of the tools. There were two big machine-shop-style band saws that Sam and Deitmar used to cut the rough wood blocks down to size. Sam spent one afternoon with a big gouger, a tool the size of a billy club, getting rid of excess wood on the one-piece maple back. The tape I'd recorded while he worked is full of the sound of him grunting heavily as he lunged at the wood. It sounds like he's in a boxing ring doing some sparring. The wood itself, being gouged away, let forth a noise that sounded uncannily like a scream.

Such rough work was a small part of the process. The carving quickly became more refined, done with smaller gougers and then a set of planes as the preliminary graduation of the thicknesses was done. The carving left less and less wood and more and more of something that looked like a violin. As work progressed to the final stages, I saw Sam working on the back with one of those thimble-size finger planes, a tool that would seem at home in a dollhouse workshop. I spent a whole afternoon watching him work on the final thickness graduation of the violin top with a scraper that removed wood not in pieces, not even in shavings, but in grains. He'd weighed the piece before he started, scraped and scraped for several hours and weighed it again when he was finished. The sum difference in his day's work was three grams.

The shrinking physical scale of the work was obvious. The expanding mental side was less so.

One day, as the violin was coming together, I arrived at the shop to find Sam with the all-but-finished top turned upside down on his worktable. Onto it he was fitting a carved piece of wood that looked a little like the tail fin of a 1950s vintage car. This was the bass-bar, another part of the fiddle that would never be seen again after the instrument was completed, a kind of support beam that is glued to the inside of the belly, running longitudinally down the front, a little to the left of the center line of the instrument, under one of the feet of the bridge that held the strings tense above it. Not only does it provide support against the pressure of the string tension, but it is also considered an important factor in creating the ultimate sound of the fiddle.

Sam had carved the bass-bar with a sharp knife, and even now, as he worked fitting the piece, he'd occasionally slice a small piece away, almost like he was whittling something. The bar was made from a piece of the old spruce Sam had bought on a trip to Europe. "I selected the wood very carefully," he told me. "It's really old stuff, and it went through the whole process we use for the top—

analyzing its density and strength and all that. Some people prefer stiffer bass-bars, but I've gone toward liking softer, lighter bars for whatever reason. I think they're a little more lively, though I couldn't prove it."

Sam had positioned the bar on the underside of the violin belly and attached it temporarily with a little clamp that had been developed by his teacher Carl Becker. I asked him to narrate what he was thinking while he worked.

"Okay," he began, "what I'm doing is I'm fitting it very carefully. There's spring to the bar. You can see that on the ends there's about three-quarters of a millimeter where it's standing up from the top." I pulled a credit card out of my wallet and asked Sam to measure the thickness with a precise caliper he used. The credit card was just about three-quarters of a millimeter.

When those ends were fitted and glued, the thicker center portion of the bass-bar would flex the violin top upward. The bar was located approximately under the lowest pitched string of the fiddle, the G. A few inches away, the sound post, a small cylindrical spruce rod, would be wedged under the bridge about where the highest pitched string— the E—is stretched.

"Spring of the bass-bar is a whole pet topic," Sam said. "At this Violin Society of America meeting where I'm going soon, it'll be very controversial. There are people who think it's an awful thing to do. It's true that it has to be done very, very carefully in order not to screw up the instrument. But I think if it's done right it makes a difference tonally, for the better.

"But at a meeting of violin makers, in some hotel ballroom, all you have to say is 'What do you think about tension in the bass-bar?' and it's like throwing a grenade into the room. I had a friend ask that question once and then he just walked out. Hours later people were still arguing."

He worked for another hour or so on the bass-bar, which looked like a couple of Popsicle sticks carved into a streamlined, aerodynamic shape. I kept imagining the scene where a whole hotel ballroom full of people shouted at one another, fighting about how this little stick should be carved and where it should be placed. While he worked, Sam talked about his theories on how the bar could change the sound of a violin, emphasizing either the lower or upper end of the frequencies, altering the responsiveness. "I don't know how much you really want to know about this," he said, several times. "I feel like I'm just starting to get an understanding of this. There could be more to know." By the time he finally glued the bar onto the top it had been dark for a while and a blustery wind had started to blow.

"It's starting to come together," Sam said on the sidewalk outside the shop as we were about to part, me for the subway back to Manhattan, him for the walk home. "It's starting to look like a fiddle."

It would be early spring by the time just about everything that didn't look like Gene Drucker's violin had been cut and gouged and scraped away. I had begun to collect discarded material which I would take home in my pocket and store in a little glass jar. There was a small section of the purfling, a stiff little sandwich of wood smaller than a toothpick. There was one of the f-hole shapes that Sam had cut into the top, the discard that gave the violin one of its most distinctive features, like an incredibly fancy doughnut hole. These two shaped pieces sat on a bed of wood shavings from both the clean spruce top and the fancier flamed maple back. A few of the shavings were broad and curled, like a sliver from a wedge of good Parmesan cheese. Most were smaller, thinner slices, like what's left when you sharpen a pencil with a knife. This was all I was going to get. As work progressed and Sam labored to perfect the fiddle, all that got scraped away was dust. Once he suggested I smell the spruce as he scraped at it, and I snorted some of what might have been Gene's fiddle as if it were cocaine.

"I'm starting to really know this wood," Sam told me one afternoon when I came into the shop. It was a dreary day with a hard, cold rain, and Sam sat at his worktable with the violin top. He'd swung the bulb of an architect's lamp directly over where he worked. He pulled a small, thin metal scraper across the wood with quick, short strokes.

"I'm in the mood to find every little place to take away more material," he said. He scraped away for a while, then lifted the wood plate off the worktable and held it near his ear. With a knuckle he tapped at the wood, keeping his ear close.

"I'm listening for a couple things," he said. "If all other factors are the same, the higher the note, the stronger the piece." A few times he whacked at his architect's lamp, because he knew that produced a certain pitch that he could use for comparison. Sometimes Sam picked up a little wooden recorder, the kind children learn to play in school, and blew a few notes, trying to match what he'd just heard from his wood plate. "My life would be simpler if I had perfect pitch," he said once.

"Besides pitch, the other thing I'm listening for," he said, "is the quality in that pitch. Does it have a full sound? Does it sustain? How hard a hit does it take to make it sound? None of this is random—there are whole schools of thought on what the pitches should be." He scraped more, tapped and listened more. "This top is very light, so my tendency is to leave it thicker. But there's a danger to leaving it too thick. And, there's also a danger in making it too thin."

At other times, after scraping for several minutes, Sam would take hold of the top in both hands and give it a twist.

"The fiddle is vibrating all over the place in all kinds of different ways," he said. "The strength of the plate is important in various dimensions. One is cross-wise flex. That's probably the most important." He twisted the top to demonstrate. I realized that I had skipped a breath, fearing that he would break the carefully carved piece in half. "It's not just important how much it moves but the type of movement. Is it a crisp response? Does it want to jump all the way back, or does it have a kind of gummy, more leathery feel to it. That softer leathery feeling could actually make a better, warmer sound. But it's not an absolute and I prefer a crisper feel, because generally it will probably give a louder, more clear-sounding instrument.

"All these tests," he said, "pitches, feel, weighing—they're not so much a guide to what I actually do; they're more warnings against doing anything weird or dangerous."

From spending time with Sam while he worked I'd come to recognize certain common themes, and the one that came up most frequently was represented by a phrase he repeated again and again: "All things being equal." He would begin an explanation like that and then go on to tell me a rule about arching, or thicknesses. Almost always, as he finished his explanation, he would conclude with another phrase: "Of course, things are never equal." There were just too many variables in the equation.

"Part of making decisions when you're building a fiddle is going from general ideas of what would probably be good to very specific details of what would be good in *this* situation. What I'm doing now is pretty fussy. But I am actually finding places to take material away. It would have been much more convenient to establish the thicknesses and never mess with it again.

"It's hard to know which is a really significant part of what you're doing and which is just an incidental part. And that's true at every stage."

For crucial parts of this violin, Sam was now within tenths of a millimeter of having everything that wasn't the Drucker violin removed for good. There was no going back, and yet there was still a lot of work to do. Some of it was what Sam would call whacking away at wood: carving the scroll, the neck, the fingerboard. He'd pop the rib structure with its blocks and linings off the mold, and eventually, after he'd worried over everything some more—maybe even removed a little more wood—he'd glue the back and belly into place.

Sam had revealed much of himself over these months. Maybe not as much as Joseph P. Reid, the guy who thought you could build a Stradivarius in your basement, would imagine. But plenty. Like it or not, Sam's character and nature were built into this box. Would it be simply average, or somehow magical? And how could you really know the difference?

Chapter 9

WHAT DO WE
REALLY KNOW?

I wish Strad had left us a little book or something," Sam Zygmuntowicz told me more than once. "Something that said, 'Make it thinner here, here, and *here*; leave it thicker there, there, and *there* and you'll get a particular sound. That would be nice. But, of course, he didn't do that."

Despite his teenage work at Zapf's in Philadelphia, his training with Peter Paul Prier, his intense summer tutorial with the esteemed Carl Becker, and his five-year boot camp apprenticeship with René Morel, Sam maintained that most of what he'd learned about building good instruments came from studying great instruments, particularly the 1716 Cessole Stradivari and Guarneri del Gesù's 1735 Plowden. "They have been like textbooks," he wrote once for *The Strad*. Textbooks "that I can study again and again. They are archetypes of great sound and style."

Yet after I'd been hanging around his workshop for several months, Sam revealed something that is an open secret among those intimate with famous old fiddles, but not very well known to most music lovers, let alone laymen. "People don't like to talk about it," Sam said, "but most Guarneris and Strads have been tampered with in one way or another."

The implications of what he said didn't seem terribly important at the time; but the more I thought about it, the stranger it seemed. Sam had used a very good, evocative analogy to explain what he meant by "tampering." "It's like those old American cars in Cuba that were there before Castro, and are still running. They're classic Chevys or Fords, but chances are that most of the parts are different." Turning this over and over in my mind, I suffered a small crisis of faith and understanding. Here I was, beginning to fully appreciate this strange, hermetic world I'd been allowed to enter. A world that seemed to contradict everything we modern Americans held dear: progress, innovation, speedy technical advance. A world where less and less meant more and more. In this world the experts seemed to agree on one thing: the work of some artisans in a small Italian town three hundred years ago might never be surpassed, and was rarely, if ever, duplicated. How could this theory, this peculiarly fascinating worldview, hold up if the work of the old guys had already been altered?

First I had to learn what had been changed on those Guarneris and Stradivaris. It turned out to be a lot.

The setting for music making in the seventeenth and eighteenth centuries was substantially different from what came later. Among the few solid facts known about Stradivari's workshop is that he filled orders from kings in France and England. The music that would be performed on these fiddles would truly be "chamber" music, concerts given by small ensembles in relatively small palace halls. The sonic requirements placed on these fiddles were light, and their sweet, light sound matched perfectly the Baroque music they were playing. But as the decades passed and a new, larger, and more democratic class of audience emerged, concert halls got larger, and with them the size of orchestras. The very music got heavier and denser. Fiddles simply needed to be louder.

Some believe it was part of Stradivari's great genius that he anticipated the change, and his later instruments were more powerful. But still not powerful enough to stay in running order for hundreds of years. Through the eighteenth and nineteenth centuries most older violins were taken apart and the original bass-bar replaced with a larger, thicker bar. The neck was lengthened and tilted at a sharper angle to allow for a longer fingering board and stronger strings at higher tension. Often, when the instruments were apart for these changes, the new craftsmen would regraduate the tops and backs. Of course, they were unable to add wood (except patches to repair worn spots or cracks); they always removed wood, making the bellies and backs thinner.

Sometimes, they considered more drastic action. The Hill brothers, while researching their book on Stradivari, found the account book of a Spanish priest who took up fiddle making in late-eighteenth-century Madrid. In one entry, the priest, Dom Vicenzo Ascensio, recounts how the curator of the Spanish Royal Court instruments brought him a Stradivari violin dated 1709, and "requested me to improve the quality of the tone, which was bad."

Padre Ascensio took the fiddle apart, made some alterations, but made a worried note in his book that his "improvements" were probably not enough. "If after this work the violin is not improved, I think it hopeless unless I put a new back and belly to it." According to the Hills, the court musicians were satisfied with what was left of the Stradivari and didn't ask for any more "improvements."

More than a century later, Sam Zygmuntowicz wrote that "the original intent of the old makers is only half the story." He then described what might be the common history of a typical Stradivari or Guarneri instrument: regraduated by the Italian makers named Mantegazza; given a longer neck by the famous French copyist Jean-Baptiste Vuillaume, who worked in Paris in the mid-1800s; patched and restored by the Hills in London just before the turn of the twentieth century; fitted again with another new bassbar by the master restorer Simone Sacconi in post–World War II New York. Where in all that retrofitting could one even find the maker's original intent?

I wondered, considering how carefully Sam had worked on his bass-bar—its carving, its placement, its controversial much-argued-over springiness—wouldn't Stradivari and Guarneri have done the same? What did it mean that, decades later, someone who wasn't Stradivari or Guarneri had pried open their masterpieces and stuck in a new bass-bar, like some Cuban mechanic putting a rebuilt carburetor into a 1958 Impala? If Sam spent so many hours, days, and years studying those old fiddles, keeping notebooks full of detailed graduation charts that looked like topographical maps—whose work was he actually analyzing?

And I thought of a game Sam liked to play when he met with his colleagues during that summer week in Oberlin. After the dinner dishes had been cleared, as the makers finished their wine, or popped open another beer and socialized a bit before returning for the evening session in the workshop, Sam would get the attention of the table and ask a simple question, yet one among his particular craft that was loaded with portent. Okay, Sam would say, getting an impish look, "What do we really know?"

I sat in on one session of What Do We Really Know? at Oberlin, and there was a lot of banter and good-natured bluster as the makers debated arching and graduation and design. (Luckily, no one threw in the loaded-grenade question about bass-bar tension.) Afterward, walking from the dining hall to the workshop in the muggy Ohio night, I asked Sam what had been concluded—What *did* they really know?

"Actually, very little," he said.

Well then, what did Stradivari really know? Though there is all that debate about exactly when and how he came to the workshop of Amati, there is no doubt that Antonio Stradivari learned his craft in the old guild tradition. Guilds kept secrets, and craftsmen trained in the system considered themselves only that—craftsmen—and not artists. In the flowering of the Renaissance, many artisans began to see themselves as individuals, as *artists*. With the development of printing in the sixteenth century, many of these artists produced treatises. The first was the Italian sculptor Ghiberti, says Jacques Barzun in his magisterial history of Europe. And, Barzun writes, "After Ghiberti's the deluge." Alberti, one of the architects of St. Peter's in Rome, left treatises on architecture, perspective, computation, and bookkeeping. Palladio wrote his famous works on building. Dürer wrote on painting and human proportions. Da Vinci compiled his notebooks. Violin making developed and reached its apotheosis in an age where all these ideas were still in the air. Yet no violin maker from the Golden Age of Cremona left behind a manual. The rules were built into the objects themselves.

The Hills also note that for a lengthy period after his death, Stradivari's instruments were not considered the epitome of sound. That distinction belonged to people like Jakob Stainer, an Austrian luthier who worked around the same time as Stradivari, or later makers who thought they had surpassed all the guys from Cremona. But somehow, as time passed, a different standard developed. It was back to the future. Though there would be a small, cult-ish group of players who preferred the Guarneri sound (a group founded by the great Paganini), they remained a subset. For a long time now, what everyone has wanted from a violin maker, no matter what they did to achieve it, was the sound of Stradivari.

But how do we really know that sound?

Despite being exceptionally difficult to talk (and write) about, sound, in a fundamental sense, is quite simple. It is air vibrating. Yet the complicated way those vibrations are produced—especially in a bowed string instrument—and the equally complicated ways those vibrations are perceived by humans give scientists from a variety of fields lifetimes' worth of work and, so far, few definitive answers. And no amount of empirical research has made hearing less personal. Sound, Sir James Beament con-cluded, in *The Violin Explained*, is "subjective and suscep-tible to suggestion, belief and myth."

So now, when listeners think they are hearing a Stra-divari, they think it is an unmatchable example of great sound. But there are plenty of examples of times when listeners, even trained experts, are just plain wrong. Such stories that I came across ranged from the most theatrical (and perhaps apocryphal) tale of how Fritz Kreisler once played an entire concert on a cheap manufactured fiddle. Of course, he was known for playing the great Guarneri that would later be named for him. As he basked in the warm applause this night, the story goes, Kreisler lifted the fiddle in the air, smashed it to pieces, and enjoyed the shocked gasps of the audience before summoning his del Gesù from the wings. You have to wonder if the audience really got what must have been the point of his theatrics. Many can recognize the sound of Kreisler, but almost no one can actually spot the sound of a great Cremonese fiddle.

More recently, David Finckel, the cellist of the Emerson Quartet, has been playing on a Zygmuntowicz copy of the famous Duport cello long played by Finckel's teacher, Mstislav Rostropovich. When the cello was finished, Finckel convinced Sam to put a fake Stradivari label inside the instrument. After concerts, when admirers came backstage to congratulate him and marvel at his instrument, Finckel would show them the Strad label. "Oh, of course," more than one music fan told him, "with that sound it had to be a Stradivari."

"I got more than a few laughs out of that," Finckel told me.

In 1963, violin maker and acoustics researcher Carleen Hutchins (one of the founders of a group of violin researchers called the Catgut Acoustical Society) wrote an article for *Scientific American* in which she reported that she had taken a five-dollar violin that was used by Harvard physicist George Saunders as "his 'standard' of badness" on his many acoustical experiments. Hutchins took the bad fiddle apart, did some adjustments, and then used it in a test with a college music department audience. Players behind a screen alternated between playing the revamped five-dollar fiddle and an "excellent Cremona violin." (Hutchins did not report its maker.) The two were judged equal in tone by the trained listeners.

Tests like this have been undertaken for a long time.

Perhaps the earliest was done in 1817 by the French National Academy. The results, according to Sir James Beament, are remarkably similar and tend to support what I began to call the Zygmuntowicz Uncertainty Principle. These tests, Beament writes, "have all produced results which one would expect from pure chance."

My favorite episode in the game of What Do We Really Know? comes from a BBC radio program from 1977, when music critic John Amos gathered together three formidable experts: violinists Isaac Stern and Pinchas Zukerman, and Charles Beare, then (and now) one of the most respected and successful violin experts and dealers in the world. Stern and Zukerman entertained millions (and made millions) playing the fiddle. On Beare's word, millions could be spent obtaining one.

For the test, the BBC had gathered four instruments. One was a later-period Stradivari, the 1725 instrument dubbed the Chaconne. One was a 1739 Guarneri del Gesù. Another was a violin made in 1846 by Vuillaume, the most respected maker of his day, and a brilliant copyist. The fourth fiddle was a little over a year old, produced by a British luthier who was actually still alive. All four would be played in the London Broadcasting House studio by a noted British soloist. He would play parts of the same two pieces on each. First, the Bruch violin concerto in G minor, whose opening allowed the player to work on all four strings of the instrument. Second, the iconic Bach Chaconne. The violins would be played behind a screen so the judges could not pick up any visual clues.

From the start they complained. Isaac Stern said the

recording studio was the wrong place to perform such a test. Charles Beare said it didn't matter what people heard in the audience, "the difference between great and good is what [the violin] does for a great player under the ear with an orchestra." Zukerman didn't have a chance to protest before John Amos gave them all a figurative pat on the hand and promised, "It's not an examination of you. We're just wondering whether one can tell immediately the tone differences."

In this case, it turns out, these two great virtuosos and one renowned expert might as well have flipped a coin to determine their opinions. No one got more than two out of four correct. And the correct guesses and wrong guesses were completely different among the three men.

The talk continued for a little while after the results. Isaac Stern strongly advised young players to work with a new instrument until they knew enough and had enough money to buy an old one. (Twenty-five years later, after he commissioned Sam Zygmuntowicz to copy each of his famous old Guarneris, Stern often lent the copies to up-and-coming young players.) John Amos tried to elicit some final lessons learned from his panel of experts. Zukerman said his Guarneri made him feel better when he was nervous. Beare, the dealer in old instruments, stuck to his guns that older was better.

Finally, as the program was running out of time, Maestro Stern said, "We hope your listeners are as pleasantly confused as we are."

Confused, to say the least. That's what I was. The world of violins began to seem like a variation of the famous tale of the emperor's new clothes. Or a strange little society where there was some form of mass hypnosis at work. Stradivaris are the greatest violins ever made because ... everybody says so. They're better because ... no one knows. They sound better ... except when they don't, or when it's not a Stradivari that you think you're hearing.

I was in the midst of all this uncertainty, trying to understand what it said about violin making that no one really knew what made great *great*, when a curator in New York threw the proverbial hand grenade into the figurative room full of violin experts. He said that he'd scientifically determined that the most famous Stradivari violin of all couldn't have been made by Stradivari.

The story of the violin known as the Messiah is perhaps the epitome of the Stradivari mystique—though mythos might be a better word.

The Messiah was made in 1716 but was still on a shelf in Stradivari's workshop when he died in 1737. As with almost everything connected to Stradivari, the reason it was never sold led to much speculation. The most romantic conclusion—and perhaps the correct one—is that the old guy knew that this was his most perfect creation in a long and distinguished career and he simply could not part with it. As the Stradivari-owning violinist and writer Joseph Wechsberg said in his entertaining and generally clear-eyed book *The Glory of the Violin*, before and after the Messiah "no better violin was ever made."

Antonio's youngest son, Paolo Stradivari, who shunned

the family business and became a merchant, didn't seem to have such reverence for the fiddle. After his father's death, he agreed to sell the violin to Count Cozio di Salabue in 1755. Though Paolo died before the transaction was complete, the count made it part of his great collection for about fifty years, until he sold it to Luigi Tarisio, the man who had become the premier collector and rescuer of Stradivari's instruments as the master's reputation faded in the decades after his death.

From there, the story gets nearly comical. Tarisio often brought his Cremona discoveries to Paris, where J. B. Vuillaume would act as a broker for resale. (And who, while the Strads were in his possession, often made copies so frighteningly exact that there are plenty of rumors that a number of instruments considered Stradivari are actually Vuillaume.) While in Paris, Tarisio spoke often of this perfect violin he had obtained—it was then named for the count who'd originally bought it: the Salabue. In fact, Tarisio mentioned this fiddle so often that one day Vuillaume's son-in-law Delphin Alard, a great violin soloist himself, had finally heard enough. "Monsieur Tarisio," Alard reportedly said, "your Stradivari is like the Messiah—he never comes."

Tarisio emulated the master maker; he died before selling the perfect violin. A solitary and miserly obsessive, he was reportedly found in a dingy Milan garret, clutching two violins (can we imagine the identity of one of them?), his cold body lying on a mattress stuffed with money he'd made over the years selling the old Cremonese masterpieces. Vuillaume was the first dealer to learn of Tarisio's death and made a quick trip to Lombardy, where he bought everything from Tarisio's survivors, including the perfect Stradivari violin, which he now named the Messiah.

Back in Paris with his find, Vuillaume did some of that Cuban mechanical work on the fiddle, lengthening the neck to put it into modern playing shape, changing the bass-bar. He probably made many copies based on its form. And though he set a price on Stradivari's masterpiece, it was always too high for a taker. The Messiah stayed in a glass case in his shop. Whether that was purposeful or not, Vuillaume, like Tarisio before him, like the great Stradivari before that, died before parting with the Messiah. Of such coincidences are legends made.

Finally, after Vuillaume's estate was settled, the Messiah became the possession of the man who'd inspired its memorable name, Delphin Alard. He already owned a Strad and didn't much care to play his new one.

The Hills bought it in 1890 for 50,000 francs, about 2,000 British pounds. After a series of sales to people who were more collectors than performers, the Messiah ended up back in the possession of the Hills. Though it had hardly been played throughout its life, the violin was perhaps the best-known instrument in England, having arrived for a show in antique instruments in 1872 and been the subject of a series of articles in the British press on the majesty of the Cremonese masters.

The two surviving Hill brothers decided that the Messiah should be kept pristine and agreed to donate the violin to the Ashmolean Museum in Oxford. (Once

again, the "curse" of this fiddle appeared; both brothers died before the legal work was done.) But eventually,
after World War II ended, the Messiah went on display
at the Ashmolean, destined to be studied and revered for
ages as the most perfectly preserved example of Antonio
Stradivari's genius.

Then, in 1997, Stewart Pollens, a New Yorker who
worked preserving the violin collection at the city's Metropolitan Museum, got permission from the Messiah's
keepers in Oxford to take some high-quality photographs
of the violin. It is a rare person who actually gets to touch
the instrument.

As Pollens later recounted it, he'd long had some sus-
picions about the authenticity of the Messiah. There was
so much legend and myth mixed into the provenance of
this fiddle that some discrepancies in the documentation
were ignored. For instance, a few of the descriptions that
Count Cozio made while he owned it didn't match those
of the Hills. Two patches inside the instrument noted by
Count Cozio were not mentioned by the Hills, who wrote
an entire monograph about the Messiah in 1882. Pollens
was not the first to question the authenticity of the Messiah. One story had it that Simone Sacconi, the legendary
twentieth-century restorer and copyist, who'd devoted
his life to studying Stradivari, had been given an audience
with the violin and declared it a copy by Vuillaume. But
decades had passed since there'd been any serious public
discussion of the Messiah and its authenticity.

That changed when Pollens sent some of those high-
resolution photos he'd taken to a German scientist,

Dr. Peter Klein, who analyzed the violin's spruce belly using the technique of dendrochronology. The growth of a tree is unique to the climatic conditions of each year it is alive, evidenced by its internal rings. Dendrochronology can compare the growth rings of a certain tree with a collected database of trees from the same region and give a surprisingly accurate date for the last year that tree lived.

Klein told Stewart Pollens that the spruce of the Messiah front had been alive in 1738. Since Stradivari died in 1737, this finding started a new—and incredibly two-fisted—game of What Do We Really Know?

While it may be true that violin makers will fight vociferously over the tension in a bass-bar, that kind of argument really is a function of caring more and more about less and less. Pollen's claim directly pointed to the validity and expertise of violin experts and dealers, a very small coterie who operated as gatekeepers to a rarefied place where top fiddles were reaching prices of nearly $5 million. There was more and more money involved, and these people cared quite a bit. If the most famous fiddle in the world had fooled all the experts, who would fully trust a dealer's appraisal again?

"When you try to move in on the world of dealers," I was told by a well-known violin maker who'd tried it once, "they'll kill you. Not literally kill you. But almost."

The charge against Pollens was led by Charles Beare, the London expert who'd so confidently told the BBC audience (after not identifying correctly half of the violins played for him) that modern makers needed to just keep trying to make them as good as the old guys. Along with the remaining heirs of the Hill family and officials at the Ashmolean, Beare enlisted two different dendrochronolgists to date the Messiah. Unsurprisingly, they were given greater access to the instrument and came back with a finding that the wood could be last dated in the 1680s, and furthermore, it matched well with the wood of other acknowledged Strads from his Golden Period in the early 1700s.

That didn't end the argument so much as kick it to a higher and more shrill level. There were intimations of a cover-up, broad intimations of incompetence from both sides, and some good old-fashioned mudslinging. Pollens, writing to an online violin Web site called Soundpost, complained about ad hominem attacks against him. The editor of the site collected all postings on the Messiah controversy under the rubric "Tree Ring Circus."

The circus, mostly, had struck its tent and moved on by the time I asked Sam about the Messiah brouhaha one day while I sat in his studio and watched him scrape away at the belly of the Drucker fiddle. Sam knew Pollens. Years before, Pollens had written a long article about Sam for *The Strad,* documenting his re-creation of a Guarneri violin. "I can't understand why he got into all this," Sam told me. "I really can't see what he had to gain from it all."

But what an exciting session it was of the ongoing game of What Do We Really Know?

"I guess," Sam said. He pushed his glasses up on his

forehead and peered intently at the spot he'd been scraping. "I know that this wood is some of the lightest I've ever worked with. It's really incredible stuff. And that's all that matters to me right now." With that Zygmuntowicz went back to his work.

Chapter 10

WE GO TO CREMONA

opping over the Swiss and Italian Alps on an early morning flight from Zurich to Milan in an uncrowded plane with a very friendly crew will easily be one of my best travel memories ever. I was on my way to Cremona. My pilgrim's progress in the violin world seemed incomplete without this pilgrimage.

When I told my fiancée that I thought it necessary to run off to Italy for research we came very close to recreating that scene in *To Kill a Mockingbird* where young Jem Finch decides to accompany his father on the grim trip to inform his client's wife that her husband is dead.

"You want me to go with you?" Jana asked me.

"No, I think I'd better go out there alone," I told her, as Atticus Finch had told his son.

"I'm goin' with you."

And that was that. Now, Jana sat beside me, sipping a rich, foamy cappuccino and marveling at the way the sun sparkled off the snow of the Alpine peaks, which were so close it seemed we could lean out of the plane and scoop up a snowball.

The next leg of our trip was a substantial comedown. Slogging our luggage through the dingy vault of the old Milan train station. Tripping through my hastily crammed traveler's Italian to get us tickets on the Mantova line. Fighting through jet lag–laden fatigue to get something to eat, trade for some euros, and catch the right train. But we were going to Cremona! I was going to walk the same cobblestones that Stradivari walked, maybe sit in the same church pew, breathe the same air, and watch the same sunset.

Sam Zygmuntowicz was not especially encouraging when I told him of this trip. He'd been to Cremona and seemed resolutely unimpressed. "You might find something of interest," he said stoically. "At least you'll eat well." But I ignored his lack of enthusiasm and sided with his colleague and rival Gregg Alf, whom I'd met at the violin makers' workshop in Oberlin. When he was young, Alf had moved to Cremona to study violin making and stayed on for eight years. Alf had written, "I felt that the spirit of Stradivari would be in the air."

After clattering through the dull industrial suburbs of Milan, the train took us eastward into countryside that turned increasingly rural and agricultural with each passing kilometer. We were in the rich, fertile floodplain of the Po River, mostly brown now in fall, but with a few brilliant patches of green here and there. Jana and I sat nervously, watching the countryside, letting the unintelligible and musical language of our fellow travelers wash over us, checking again and again with the conductor.

Cremona?

Not yet.

I decided to distract myself with the book I'd been rereading on the transatlantic flight. Just before I began this whole project I'd taken a short trip to New Orleans and met a doctor there who played violin seriously. When I told him that I was about to see how a violin is built, he told me forcefully: "You have to read *The Violin Hunter*." It turned out to be a good prescription.

The book is a historical biographical novel by William Alexander Silverman, who wrote it in 1957. The violin hunter of the title is Luigi Tarisio, who had died owning the Messiah. Starting as a poor itinerant carpenter and dance fiddler, Tarisio dedicated his life to rediscovering and collecting the then-neglected violins of Cremona's Golden Age.

Now locked in a shabby second-class train car, I retraced the journey Tarisio had made on foot in the mid-1820s, wandering from his home in Milan toward Cremona, doing odd jobs for his bed and supper, hoping to fiddle at a dance, shrewdly stopping at monasteries where he knew he could find not only a charitable host, but also perhaps some dusty fiddles commissioned more than a hundred years before.

However he did it, wherever he found them, Luigi Tarisio appeared in Paris in 1827 with a sack full of old violins. Legend has it that he had walked all the way from Italy, carrying the trove of masterpieces on his back. He was rough around the edges, but Tarisio knew enough to search out the leading violin makers and dealers of the day—M. Aldric, Georges Chanot, and Jean-Baptiste Vuillaume.

With the appearance of these previously unknown fiddles, word spread through Paris quickly. During his visit, Tarisio provided Paganini with the del Gesù that would become his lifelong love, an instrument so powerful it was called the Cannon. Leaving behind several Stradivaris, a Bergonzi, and a couple violins by lesser-known Cremonese, the violin hunter returned to Milan with a wallet stuffed with francs to finance and renew his search. Over the years he unearthed scores of Cremonese instruments and became a primary agent in rebuilding Stradivari's reputation.

There has been plenty of revisionist work on the biography of Tarisio. It's commonly accepted that he placed fake Stradivari labels in lesser instruments, though he hardly started that practice and would certainly not be the last culprit to do so. Tarisio took the credo "Buy low, sell high" very seriously, and probably cheated some unknowing Italians out of valuable pieces. But Silverman paints a warm-hued portrait of the man, lanky and plain, unlucky at love, committed to the old violins with a nearly religious fervor. As our train finally pulled into Cremona, I looked up at the tall bell tower of the Torrazzo attached to the town's main cathedral, the inevitable first view one gets of the town. You can't miss it; Cremona is a low-built provincial place, and the Torrazzo is the tallest bell tower in Europe. I realized that I now shared one small experience with Tarisio and, come to think of it, many of the legends of the violin world.

We waited near the grim, dirty train station—it spoke of Mussolini more than Stradivari—for Patricia Kaden, whom I'd retained to guide us through the city and its cache of violin lore. A French Canadian by birth, she'd lived in Paris for a while, then landed in Cremona more than a decade before my visit with a husband who'd decided to become a violin maker and wanted to go to the source. He was no longer in Cremona, but Patricia had stayed on and used her affinity for fiddles and trilingual skills to help folks like me. She advertised her services in a few violin journals, so I'd heard of her, but it was a violin maker I'd met at Oberlin who had convinced me I should hire Patricia. "She knows the town," he'd told me. "Not just the violins, but the restaurants and cafés."

Patricia arrived pushing a big old bicycle. She was a small woman in latter middle age, friendly and attractive, with a propensity for walking. "No need for a cab," she said, "follow me." We wheeled and dragged our luggage through uneven streets and over stone sidewalks for what seemed like an hour until we finally reached the Palazzo Cattaneo, the ancestral home of Duke Cattaneo, a dashing man (Patricia whispered that he'd enjoyed a reputation as a European playboy in his day) who'd turned the palazzo into something of an artists' colony. We climbed four narrow, twisting flights of stairs to an attic suite with a giant wood beam just high enough to stand under in the parlor, a beautiful marble bath, and a small bedroom. "I love it," Jana said. "It's ancient." That seemed worth the fifty euros a night we were being charged.

"You probably want to rest a little," Patricia said. "But come tonight and join us for *aperitivo* at six or so. You'll meet some people."

It is estimated that there are now more violin makers working in Cremona than there were in all the years from the first Amati through Bergonzi, when the violin's design and construction was being developed and perfected. That's probably an estimation uttered with some sarcasm; but when Jana and I arrived for drinks that evening at a bustling little alley café called the Bar Bolero, Patricia handed me a printed list of luthiers in town. It went alphabetically from Katarina Abbuhl to Nicola Zurlini—ninety-eight listings. Many of the listings were firms where several partners worked. So there were well over a hundred violin makers plying their trade in Cremona at the dawn of the twenty-first century.

Even after just a few hours in town, it was easy to see what attracted them. Cremona was a charming place. When the sun went down and the mist rolled in from the Po, there seemed to be an otherworldly quality to the old city. If you let your imagination run just a little, it was easy to feel that Stradivari's spirit was indeed in the air.

There was also a very practical lure: the International School of Violin Making, the only school of its kind in Italy, which offers a five-year program that awards a diploma as a master of violin making. Italian kids could enter the school at the age of fourteen and earn their high school diploma and the technical degree. Over the years, the school has attracted a large number of foreign students, most of whom, like Gregg Alf, arrive in Italy as adults. Alf, I would learn, was still something of a legend in Cremona for driving around town in a Jaguar convertible. The local police would stop him all the time—not to arrest him, but just to marvel at the big engine.

The school was born, not coincidentally, in 1938, a year after the two-hundredth anniversary of Stradivari's death. In 1937, the city of Cremona hosted a celebration and exhibition dedicated to the city's most famous son. The popularity of the event convinced the Mussolini government (reportedly, Il Duce himself was fond of fiddles) that there was good public relations potential in reviving the Italian violin making tradition. The school's founders offered the directorship to Simone Sacconi, the Roman-trained luthier who'd helped organize the Stradivari exhibition. He turned down the job. He had recently moved to New York, where it wasn't long before he became the widely acknowledged master of violin restoration at the famed House of Wurlitzer, and fanatical devotee of Stradivari. But Sacconi would not forget Cremona.

No one interested in violins could forget Cremona. However, for many years Cremona had forgotten its illustrious cadre of luthiers. Most glaring was the town's neglect of Stradivari.

In 1869 the church where Antonio and his second wife were buried, San Domenico, was torn down, and the bones from the burial vaults were mixed and unidentified and supposedly reburied by workmen somewhere outside of town. (There is some suspicion that they simply dumped the bones in the Po.) Stradivari's house and workshop had survived into the 1920s, by which time the rooms that saw the supreme mastery of the luthier's art had become a tailor shop and a pool hall. The government replaced it with an office building just before the great Depression.

In the accumulated literature devoted to Strad, nearly every violin fanatic who makes the trek to Cremona writes a sad report of neglect. In *The Glory of the Violin*, Joseph Wechsler, who arrived in 1948, wrote, "Like other pilgrims I found nothing at all. The houses where they lived had disappeared. No streets were named after them. There was not even a great Cremonese violin left in the city where they had been created." Wechsler found a sixth-generation descendant of the master, a lawyer named Mario Stradivari, who complained that he hadn't even been invited to the great exhibition of 1937. The city's leading expert on Stradivari at the time, Renzo Bacchetta, explained to Wechsler that Cremona was simply a provincial town understandably fixated on what supported its citizens. "They cared only that the price of cheese should stay up," Wechsler reported. "If Stradivari had invented a new kind of cheese, they would have built him a monument."

Somehow, Mussolini's government had changed all that, and now Cremona held a significant number of people who revered Stradivari. I met about a dozen my first night there.

On our first visit to the Bar Bolero, Patricia introduced Jana to the charms of the dry sparkling wine called *prosecco*. I stayed stalwart to my crude American habit of drinking whiskey before dinner. A sample of some fresh local cheeses made me understand why someone might want to monumentalize the makers. Through the evening violin makers came and went. Over the years I have hung around a number of bars that catered to a particular clientele—cops, musicians, journalists, actors, people who worked in other bars—but I'd never even imagined there could be a watering hole where you could be sure to meet a violin maker. One, a small man named Toto who wore a jaunty hat and scarf, invited us to visit his workshop whenever we liked. Another, Marco, a solidly built guy with a high forehead and dark, piercing eyes, chatted formally with us for a few moments and then moved away. I glanced in his direction a little while later and found him staring at me, and not in a friendly way.

I talked mostly with Franz, a foppish thin man who'd worked as a violin maker in Cremona for many years. He was just back for a visit, since he'd recently moved to Zurich, where he was playing guitar with a band that performed the gypsy jazz music made popular by Django Reinhart. "As a violin maker I had to deal with these musicians all the time," he told me. "They just drove me crazy. I got so sick of musicians that I decided to become one."

As Sam Zygmuntowicz had predicted, that night we ate quite well.

The next morning I got out early with a map, trying to make a quick survey of sites that the town had created to counteract its reputation for neglecting Antonio Stradivari. Cremona on a weekday morning had a comfortable small-town feel, as shopkeepers performed their opening rituals, parents dropped their children at schools, workmen patched some of the old streets. I felt like the only tourist in the whole city.

I wandered through the labyrinth of the old town, where the streets crisscrossed each other in a grid-defying maze. Across the via Plasio, left on the via Cavollatti, then I realized I was lost. After backtracking on via Mazinni and a shortcut through the vaulted walkways of the Galleria—there I was at the Piazza Roma, a small park that contained the symbolic tomb of Antonio Stradivari. It was a slab of red-hued marble, about the size of a coffin, sitting off on the side of a walking path. On top of the red marble was a white marble re-creation of the carved plaque from Strad's original crypt. The whole thing looked more like a resting bench than a monument. I stared at the "tomb" for a time, knowing that there was just about nothing there that was really connected to Stradivari. The monument looked forlorn and neglected. It seemed to embody an almost complete lack of significance. Then I unfolded my map and headed for the Piazza Stradivari.

Though it was a few short blocks from the heart of Cremona—the bustling Piazza di Commune—the Piazza Stradivari was a barren field of stone blocks, bordered by some of Cremona's more modern buildings, all of them giving off the strong scent of government bureaucracy. In the midst of the otherwise empty plaza stood a statue that, from a distance, looked like two vaguely human forms, man and boy. Unfortunately, from close up it looked nearly exactly the same—some form of man looking at some form of violinlike object held up to him by some form of child. Though one small detail of Stradivari's daily life has been passed down through the generations—he always wore a white leather shop apron—the sculptor ignored that fact and clad the master in an elaborate cape. This was the town's tribute to Stradivari. I couldn't shake the following thought from my head: someone important in Cremona had a nephew who was a sculptor. I made my way back to the Palazzo Cattaneo to pick up Jana, hoping that our afternoon search to find the spirit of Stradivari would yield better results.

That afternoon, Patricia led us down the hushed halls of the Museo di Stradivari and into a big room filled with glass display cases and painted with a trompe l'oeil technique that made the simple flat walls seem like elaborately carved marble interiors of a palace. An ornate glass chandelier hung from the ceiling. The bizarre elegance seemed at odds with what the display cases held: stuff that had survived from Stradivari's workshop and the few little tidbits of documentation on his life. Astonishingly, the museum dedicated to the world's greatest violin maker didn't have one violin.

There was the bill for his first wife's funeral. He'd gone all out, hiring more than a hundred priests and fathers of various denominations (heavy on the Franciscans and Dominicans) to celebrate the mass, procuring big and little bells to be rung, retaining a corps of gravediggers with capes. Maybe the old guy was truly heartbroken. Perhaps he just felt the need to maintain appearances in a town where people spoke of being "rich as Stradivari." The historian who found these documents told the Hills that Francesca Feraboschi Stradivari's funeral was "probably among the most conspicuous of the time."

Across the room, another case held the famous letter Strad sent a client apologizing for the delay in delivering a violin—the varnish simply needed more time to dry. I had read the translation of this letter in any number of books and articles about Stradivari. Finally seeing the real item made me understand better why the profound lack of raw material had led to such extreme speculation about nearly everything connected with the man. In the wake of the masterpieces he created, there was a gaping void left by the scant and mundane stuff that has survived from his life. The experts and the acolytes could study his violins with the fervor of religious fanatics. But the only documentary evidence left from his life gave little more insight into the man than the fact that Antonio Stradivari was a lousy speller.

Delving deeper into this strangely static room, we stared into more cases that held faded drawings of f-holes, scrolls, and necks—Strad's templates for his work. There were calipers and cutting tools, several instrument molds that looked very similar to those I'd seen in Sam Zygmuntowicz's workshop, except the unvarnished wood of the master's forms was now aged and brown. The place reminded me, unfortunately, of the first museum I'd ever visited when I was a kid in Scranton, Pennsylvania. The Everhart Museum had glass cases just like the ones I now viewed, filled with a carefully arrayed collection of dead moths. It was a cultural experience that stripped all the fun from getting out of school for an afternoon. The way the curators of Cremona presented the workshop materials of their genius native son had all the sweep and grandeur of a collection of dead moths. Months after I had returned from this trip to Italy, I read a sentence in another book that perfectly captured the essence of the Museo di Stradivari. Victoria Finlay, in her wonderful *Color: A Natural History of the Palette*, writes of visiting Cremona searching for Stradivari's "secrets" with varnish pigments. Of the odd, stuffy, stultifying Museo dedicated to him, she decided, "It must qualify as one of the most boring museums about an interesting subject in the whole of Europe."

All the artifacts in the collection had been sold in the mid-1700s by Stradivari's last surviving son, the cloth merchant Paolo Stradivari, to Count Cozio di Salabue, who was building a collection of violins reputed to be the greatest ever assembled. When Count Cozio died, what was left of his collection ended up in the hands of his descendants. The Stradivari shop paraphernalia was sold in the early twentieth century to a Roman violin maker named Giuseppe Fiorini. Fiorini donated the material to the city of Cremona in 1930, so it was available for the big exhibition in 1937. After that, the stuff ended up in what the town fathers named the Museum of Organology on the third floor of the Palazzo dell'Arte. "This was a most unhappy location," according to Francesco Bissolatti, a Cremona native who became a violin maker by going through the town's international school in the 1950s. Bissolatti set up a shop in town and taught at his alma mater for years.

In 1958, Simone Sacconi came back to Cremona for the first time since the exhibition he'd helped organize twenty years before. He was now an eminence in the violin trade. He met Francesco Bissolatti, and the two luthiers became quick friends. When Sacconi saw the Stradivari workshop relics he lamented the haphazard way they were kept—"Everything denoted negligence and disinterest," according to Bissolatti, who wrote a remembrance of his mentor after Sacconi died. Sacconi convinced his young Cremonese violin maker friend to help him put the collection into better shape.

Sacconi had an intuition that in these dusty workshop materials lay the key to fully understanding Stradivari's methods. "Those molds and designs," Bissolatti remembered later, "were for [Sacconi] living testimony of the sublime art of that insuperable master." Starting in 1962, Sacconi came to Cremona nearly every year during his vacation from the House of Wurlitzer in New York. He once gave a course in restoration at the International School. He visited the local churches, following a hunch he had that the artisans who made the elaborate wood-carvings in the churches were linked somehow to the artisans who built fiddles. Bissolatti, who'd given Sacconi keys to his shop, would arrive for work at 7 A.M. to find that his friend had already been working for two hours, perhaps on an experiment with the raw materials of varnish, trying to rediscover Stradivari's technique.

The tall, cultured, and gentle Sacconi had begun to build what would be the capstone of his career, of his whole life really, since he had almost totally devoted it to violins. He was writing a book that would decode and decipher the techniques of the great Maestro of Cremona. As much as anyone could, Sacconi would create that longed-for treatise that Stradivari never left behind. He finished it just before he died, after his last visit to Cremona, in 1972, and called the book *I "Segreti" di Stradivari—The "Secrets" of Stradivari*.

"*I 'Segreti' di Stradivari* was Simone Sacconi's final gift to his profession," wrote the London dealer Charles Beare, who had worked with Sacconi as an apprentice in the House of Wurlitzer workshop. "It has become almost a bible."

I had a bootlegged copy of *The "Secrets"* that Sam Zygmuntowicz had obtained while in violin making school. Though it is possible to get a little stuck when Sacconi's writing starts to care more and more about less and less, there is still more life in those pages than in that room full of artifacts in Cremona. As might be expected from the life work of a craftsman who had unusual concentration, Sacconi's book ranges widely in explaining something very specific. He devotes much space to analyzing the mathematical principles that guided Stradivari's design of his forms and the more decorative scroll. (The scroll design, he said, combines two early mathematical discoveries: the Archimedian spiral and the spiral of Vignola.) Sacconi gives over page after page to analysis of the various archings and thicknesses in Strad's instruments. He includes a detailed discussion of the master's varnishing technique, which had become subject to the most fanciful speculation of "secret" techniques and recipes.

Sacconi's conclusion is either surprising, or perfectly obvious, depending on how much stock you put into the various Stradivari myths. The tip might have come from those quote marks around the word *Segreti* in the title. It turns out that Sacconi had labored all those years, studied all those instruments as carefully as anyone ever could, tested recipes, built impeccable copies, and in the end decided ... *there were no secrets*. Yes, some of the techniques had been "lost" over time. The continuity of tradition stopped when the long chain of master-to-apprentice teaching broke within a generation of Stradivari's death. But, Sacconi decided, Stradivari was no more—or less—than the best that ever was.

"Stradivari was not the trustee or the discoverer of any particular secret," Sacconi wrote in the last paragraph of *The "Secrets."* "To insist in such a superficial or closed vision of his personality or his work means, more than anything else, to destroy its value and to reduce him to the level of an empirical though lucky practitioner or quack. He was Stradivari because his creations were [*sic*] united the knowledge of mathematics and nature, together with a deep spirit of reflection and research, artistic sensibility, exceptional technical ability, experience and tradition."

I got out of the Museo di Stradivari about as quick as I could. Just an hour later I found myself peering into yet another glass case in Cremona. It had begun to seem that *everything* was in a glass case in this town. I began to imagine that, sooner or later, if I just kept looking, I'd come across a case with the spirit of Stradivari inside because it certainly was not in the air. The latest glass case was on the second floor of the Civic Museum, a beautiful salon with real and highly polished marble, located in Cremona's twelfth-century city hall. Inside was a gorgeous yellow-hued fiddle that Stradivari had built in 1715. It had been named the Joachim, for its former owner, Joseph Joachim, one of the greatest virtuosos of all time. Now, since it was the only violin owned by his hometown, it was dubbed the Cremonese. I walked around the case to examine the highly flamed maple of the back and ribs, the distinctive and expertly carved scroll, the sweeping curves of the outline. It was a beautiful fiddle. Perhaps this was as close as I would come to finding the spirit of the master.

Two guards armed with automatic weapons watched carefully as I pointed to the case and tried to explain to Jana how the old guy had joined the purfling corners into the classic "bumblebee stingerette."

"Oh yeah," she said, "I see that. That's really cool."

"You do?"

"Yeah, why?"

"Nothing."

We moved slowly again around the glass box. Displayed this way, the Cremonese was more a work of art than a tool. It finally registered with me why so many violinists are upset when yet another old Italian instrument is purchased by a collector or museum and becomes less and less heard and more and more simply seen. The Cremonese had six companions in identical glass cases throughout the room. There was a highly decorated fiddle that the original Cremonese master, Andrea Amati, made for Charles IX of France in 1566. There was a later Amati viola, and a violin by Nicolò Amati (who taught young Antonio Stradivari). There were two Guarneri fiddles, one by the Giuseppe known as "Giuseppe son of Andrea," and another by his more famous son Giuseppe, known as del Gesù. And last was an elaborately inlaid fiddle that looked remarkably like it had been built by Stradivari, because it was actually an impeccable copy of Strad's 1687 violin known as the Hellier, crafted by Simone Sacconi. Sacconi built it here in Cremona, right around the time he was being named an honorary citizen of the town.

Each violin was beautiful in its own way, but each, locked in its case, seemed suspended in time and somehow lifeless. I realized that I had struck up an odd and somewhat privileged relationship with violins, particularly for someone who didn't actually play. Lurking around Sam's studio, I'd been able to see and touch and hear a Stradivari and a Guarneri del Gesù. Though I was careful and reverent—always aware of how valuable they were—I'd developed a sense that they were tools made to be used. Like those classic cars rolling through the streets of Havana, they'd been ministered to all these decades to keep them alive, so that they could be driven. "I'd love to hear what these fiddles sound like," I told Jana.

Soon our guide Patricia caught up with us. She had been here so many times that the guards who'd been so stern with us (we were the only visitors) relaxed visibly, greeted her warmly, and began to chat and chuckle.

"It's too bad we weren't here earlier," Patricia told me. "They tell me that Maestro Mosconi was in today. He comes and plays the violins to keep them in shape." Toby Faber, in the process of researching his delightful book *Stradivari's Genius*, had stumbled into this museum just in time for one of Maestro Mosconi's routine concerts. Mosconi is employed by the city to keep its fiddle collection in playing condition. He generally plays one violin each day, meeting the responsibilities of what might just be the cushiest government job in the history of government jobs. Though Faber heard wrong notes and thought the playing "faintly plodding," it was also the first time he'd been so near a Stradivari being played.

"There really is something about its tone," Faber wrote later. "Warm and vibrant, it seems to inhabit the room." I remembered that Sam Zygmuntowicz had recounted a similar experience, when the soloist Daniel Heifetz visited the Violin Making School of America in Salt Lake City during Sam's first year there and played some of Bach's Chaconne on his Strad in a small room filled with prospective luthiers. It was Sam's first time hearing one of the old guy's instruments close up. "I'll never forget that sound," Sam told me.

These violins in the Palazzo Communale were beautiful. They were well treated and well guarded. But mostly they were mute, and that seemed kind of sad.

It was late afternoon by the time we left the town hall, and Jana and I both craved coffee and some gelato from a shop we'd discovered across the square. Patricia had other errands to run. Before she left us, she handed me a business card of a restaurant named Alfredo's. "You're invited to a party there tonight."

When we arrived at Alfredo's it was nearing the end of what had obviously been a boisterous *aperitivo* time. The place was packed, and we had to shoulder our way to the bar. The party was celebrating the fifth anniversary of the restaurant, and dinner would be on the house. The owner, Mario, was bartending right then, and when I asked him for Scotch on the rocks he shouted out, "Ah, the Americans are here!" Jana tried to fool him by using her most useful three words of Italian—*Prosecco, per favore*—but her Texas accent gave her away.

Soon we were seated at a bunch of small tables that had been pushed together, and Jana ended up next to the violin maker named Marco, who had seemed so cool the other night at Bar Bolero. I tried to get her attention and discreetly suggest she change seats, but it didn't work. Of course, I needn't have worried, because by the time the main course arrived—the most delicious roast pork I have ever eaten—Jana and Marco were new best friends, and he was laughing loudly and dispensing wine in copious amounts.

Patricia brought along a young French woman named Silvie, who had recently arrived from Paris and enrolled in Cremona's violin making school. Silvie had just finished carving her first scroll, and she pulled it from her bag with a mixture of pride and trepidation. She obviously was a long way from thinking, as Sam Zygmuntowicz did, that this task was simply "whacking away at wood." The scroll was unvarnished and seemed very light as it passed through my hands for a quick inspection on its way around the table. It was clear that the final judge would be Marco.

The maestro held the scroll up to the lights, turned it several times, brought it back close to his face, and peered at it down the length of his long, classic Italian nose. He had reverted to looking stern and serious. Jana glanced nervously between him and Silvie, who, when I looked at her, seemed to be deciding whether to laugh or cry.

Finally, Marco declared, *"Bene!"* and laughed, sparking an eruption of laughter at the table, which had become a small silent spot in the noisy room. Then he switched to English and said, "Everybody has to carve their first scroll." That brought a spontaneous toast at the table. This seemed like a typical moment in Cremona, which made me realize how untypical it would be anywhere else on earth. Yes indeed, everybody has to carve their first scroll. *"C'ent Anni!"* Marco passed the scroll back to Silvie and set out to refill everyone's wineglass.

I started talking to Silvie about Cremona's violin making school. We'd visited one morning—or *tried* to visit—but found there was nobody around who could give us permission to go in, but by the same token, there was nobody who cared to stop us either. I had found a young Italian student who spoke about as much French as I did, and he invited us to visit a classroom workshop. There was no sign of any teachers; a handful of students carved away at fiddles, listened to rock and roll, and smoked cigarettes. Silvie told me she was learning a lot.

When next I looked over at Jana, she and Marco were each wearing those things you clip on your head with springs that stick up like antennae. These had shiny red hearts that wiggled and bobbed as they moved their heads. By the time we got up to leave, everyone had taken a turn wearing the bobbing hearts. Before we began to try to weave our way back to what we'd taken to calling "our palazzo," I remembered to ask how much we owed for the wine. Marco shouted, "*Niente*. Nothing. *Va bene*."

"That means, 'Go well,'" he added. Marco stood and raised his glass toward us. "Come to our workshop tomorrow. Patricia will bring you."

The workshop where we went to meet Marco the next morning could have been created by a set designer. Occupying the ground-floor corner of an old stone building on the via Millazo, it had wood-paneled walls and tall, shuttered windows that looked out on a street scene which, except for the cars, seemed to be a view shared by Stradivari himself. Worktables lined three of the walls, each with an architect's lamp like the one Sam used for illumination and sounding a pitch. The standard tools—planes, gougers, scrapers, calipers—were arranged neatly, either lined up near the worktable or hung on the paneled walls. Some wood shavings dotted the tile floors. The place smelled of freshly cut spruce and varnish.

When Patricia had picked us up at our palazzo she told us, "You should be very honored that you are getting an appointment with Maestro Bissolatti." It turned out that Marco was the son of Francesco Bissolatti, who decades before had befriended Simone Sacconi. When we arrived, Marco got up from his workbench and stepped past two other workers to greet us. It was hard not to imagine him wearing two bouncy heart-shaped antennae. He took us over to a bench across the room where a gray-haired man with thick glasses and a beard was working in a blue shop apron. This was his father. Francesco welcomed us with a friendly formality and went back to work. Marco took us back across the room to his bench and introduced us to the other workers, who were his younger brothers, Maurizio and Vincenzo. Before we would leave the shop that day Marco would give me a handsome book he had written about the tradition of Cremonese craftsmanship called *The Genius of Violin Making in Cremona*. It includes chapters devoted to the Amatis, the Guarneris, the Stradivaris, the often overlooked Ruggeris and Bergonzis, and, yes, the Bissolattis. It seems Francesco has set himself up as the modern patriarch of Cremonese violin making, a new old guy, with his sons laboring nearby, the start of a new tradition. "Finally," Marco writes in the chapter

devoted to his own family, "people have begun to understand that string instruments worthy of the great Cremonese tradition are once again being made in Cremona."

We went from bench to bench and checked the instruments under construction. Maurizio, working on a viola,
seemed a bit distracted and annoyed by our being there.
Vincenzo was quite shy, but held up an unfinished fiddle
for us to admire. In another corner an older man with a
full head of gray hair worked with his back to us, and we
were not brought to his bench.

"Who's that?" Jana asked.

"He is not here," Marco said. We both looked to Patricia to see if we'd missed something that she could
translate for us. She stepped closer and whispered to us,
"That is Maestro Mosconi, the man who plays the city's
violins. But he doesn't want anyone to know he's here."
I didn't quite understand what the big deal was, but I
promised I would keep *I Segreti di Mosconi* just as long
as I could.

We turned in the other direction and entered a smaller
varnishing room, where a number of fiddles hung by
their scrolls on wires stretched horizontally at a height
that kept them just within reach, drying in the muted
sunlight. Against one wall was a table nearly covered by
jars and bottles filled with viscous varnishes, their colors
ranging from deep burgundy to nearly lemony yellow.
Jana pointed to a small cot in the corner, covered with a
blanket that pictured a polar bear, a blanket for a child.
"Who uses that?" she asked. Marco spoke Italian.

"Maestro Bissolatti," Patricia translated, "has a sacred

nap each afternoon here with the drying violins." I'd read somewhere of a legend that Stradivari had done the same thing, and some thought he meant to impart his spirit into the fiddles.

Marco shepherded us from the varnish room and through a door into a large and ornate reception area. He went to get a copy of his book, and Jana and I both gasped when we noticed a huge bronze statue looming behind us. It was Stradivari and the apprentice boy, almost the same statue I'd seen in the Piazza Stradivari, except that the figures were rendered more realistically. They actually looked like people.

"How did you get this?" I asked Marco, a little incredulous.

"It was *secondi*—runner-up in the contest. My father bought it. This one is better. The one they put in the piazza—it looks like people from another planet."

It occurred to me later: that's about the only theory that hasn't been launched to explain Stradivari's greatness.

Finally we came back to Papa Francesco's bench, and he put aside his work to talk for a few minutes. He didn't seem comfortable trying to interpret my English, so Patricia would put my questions into Italian. But then he would answer in English. It seemed a lot was getting lost in that process. For instance, when I asked what it had been like growing up around Cremona and wanting to be a violin maker, he responded in English: "Parma has cheese, we have violins!"

"How about your friend Sacconi, did he get it right?"

"A great man. A genius. Not Stradivari, but as good as anyone else."

"So," I said, "you agree with Sacconi, that there was no secret."

Francesco Bissolatti required no translation for that. "One secret," he responded immediately, holding up a finger. "The secret," he said, "is being able to do it."

This was as close as I would get to finding the spirit of Stradivari in Cremona. It was a spirit of practicality and practice. It was the spirit that propelled a man to labor for seven or eight decades at the same craft, every working day constricted by that craft's traditions, which, paradoxically, also meant being utterly free to experiment. Simone Sacconi wrote that "this craftsmanship had become a myth because it was not understood." But he hoped that his life's work, his book, would help violin makers to understand "the simple truth of a daily routine of work and of the use of techniques which contained nothing mysterious."

We said good-bye to all the Bissolattis and thanked them for their hospitality. We even said good-bye to the man who wasn't there. Marco led us out through the formal reception room, and we got one more look at the Master of Cremona, portrayed in bronze. I was going back to the shop in Brooklyn, where I knew Sam would soon be reaching the stage in making the Drucker violin that had always been the most mysterious of all.

Chapter 11

VARNISHES
AND VERY
CURIOUS SECRETS

FOR VIOLIN MAKERS, VARNISH IS LIKE SEX
OR MONEY: A DEFINING CHARACTERISTIC OF
ONE'S PERSONALITY THAT IS NOBODY
ELSE'S BUSINESS.

—*Sam Zygmuntowicz*

y April, with a little more than a month until Gene Drucker's birthday and his promised delivery date, Sam had the Drucker violin nearly built. The "box"—ribs, belly, and back—was complete "in the white," the violin making term for a fiddle that is fully carved and scraped and has the light colored hue of new wood in a lumber yard because no varnish has been applied yet. Some more woodwork needed to be done. As he prepared to carve the neck and fingerboard, Sam e-mailed Gene to see if the violinist would like the neck made to the same specifications of his Stradivari, or if he could carve his standard Zygmuntowicz neck, which was very similar, but not an exact match. "We can always reshape the neck later," Sam wrote, "but I'd like to get it right the first time."

Drucker was touring Europe with the Emerson Quartet when he got the message. He responded that he was comfortable with his Strad neck but that he didn't normally pay a lot of attention to that detail. He did send Sam detailed information on what strings he was using, expressing a willingness to experiment with different strings on the new violin. Gene concluded his reply by writing, "I'm getting excited as the time approaches for a new violin-playing experience!"

So the violin maker got out his cutting tools and carved away everything that didn't look like a neck and fingerboard for *this* fiddle. He attached the scroll and carved box that holds the pegs for string tuning to the top of the neck, and then put the whole apparatus onto the body of the violin. Now the new Drucker violin was ready to go through the process that has intrigued and confounded luthiers for centuries—varnishing.

The Hill brothers, in their grand treatise on Stradivari, begin the chapter on varnish like this: "It is with considerable diffidence that we approach the much discussed subject.... We hope to place the matter before our readers in a truer light than that in which it has hitherto appeared, and thus to dispel much of the mystery in which the subject has been involved by the ever-ready pens and fluent tongues of the many self-constituted authorities."

I think what the brothers were trying to say in their polite Victorian diffidence was—Let's cut the bull. Though the Hills tried to dispel the long-held notion of some secret varnish recipe used by Stradivari, they couldn't stop themselves from intimating at its tantalizing possibility.

The Hills wrote of repeated discussions they'd had with a descendant of the master, one Giacomo Stradivari, who claimed that as a child he'd opened an old family Bible and found handwritten on a flyleaf a recipe for the perfect violin varnish and instructions on how to apply it. Giacomo said the date of the inscription was 1704, the beginning of Strad's Golden Period. He had copied it out of that Bible, which was later lost. Though a number of people—including Jean-Baptiste Vuillaume—offered Giacomo a lot of money to share the transcribed recipe, he always demurred, saying that he would keep it to himself in case anyone in the Stradivari family decided to take up the craft again. It would give his kin an immediate competitive advantage. Giacomo Stradivari died before the Hills completed their book, and no recipe was ever found. Perhaps Giacomo had just been having fun and the story of the recipe was a hoax; perhaps it was a great loss for luthiers.

Brushing aside their tantalizing brush with "the secret," the Hills concluded that Antonio Stradivari simply did with varnish what he did in all other aspects of his craft: practiced the traditional techniques that had been handed down to him, but did it with such single-minded devotion and skill that the final result was, as the Hills liked to say, ne plus ultra. Even for the cautious and conservative Englishmen, Strad's varnish inspired some paroxysms of prototypical fiddle porn. Like this passage from their book describing the varnish of Stradivari's best instruments: "Lightness of texture, and transparency combined with brilliant yet subdued coloring ... picturesque and attractive in the highest degree."

It was commonly accepted, though, that *something* was lost within a generation or so after Stradivari's death. The Cremonese way of varnishing disappeared for several reasons. Primary was the fact that the master-apprentice chain was broken in the town where the trade had reached its apotheosis. The Hills believed that within that Cremonese tradition, each practitioner had his preferences and tricks. They could be called secrets, but they were open secrets. The real problem in matching the work of the masters was that "the spirit of artistic emulation which existed in Cremona ... had died out." To revive it would require historical detective work, retracing steps back to the original techniques.

That is exactly what Simone Sacconi did relentlessly for six decades of the twentieth century. When Sacconi was writing *his* treatise, the subject of varnish still attracted as many "ever-ready pens and fluent tongues." Much had been written and discussed and guessed at in those hundred years that passed between the two great studies of Stradivari. The depth and complexity of the research was greatly expanded by modern chemical analyses, which yielded lots of data but no definitive answers. Lingering still was a sense that when it came to varnishing, there was a holy grail just waiting to be found.

Sacconi knew all this and seemed to understand the

common human need to fill in blank spaces with elaborate doodling. "Since the luthiers and the antique traders of the last century were unable to explain the quality of the sound of Stradivari's instruments," Sacconi wrote, "they told stories of unknowable secrets."

On the last day of April, which began as a gray spring morning with a strong damp wind, I showed up at Sam's workshop to find the chair at his workbench empty. Wiltrud was working at her spot nearby with her usual concentration. When she finally noticed me she pointed toward the small room at the far left corner of the shop—the varnishing room. In my many days at the workshop, I'd only stuck my head inside that room once, on my initial tour of the place. As much as I'd studied the Hills' and Sacconi's books and accepted their debunking of the legends and mysteries surrounding Strad's varnish, as I tapped on the closed door it was difficult not to feel that I was asking to be let into a chamber full of secrets.

Sam was wearing his usual cool weather outfit—flannel shirt, dark chinos, and sandals on top of heavy socks. He had on a shop apron, which I'd only seen him wear a few times before. The room was bright but cramped, with shelves and tables loaded with jars of different colored liquids. There was a small worktable with the requisite architect's lamp clamped on the corner. Two large cabinets loomed on either side of where Sam was perched on a stool. One was an old mahogany armoire; the other a homemade beech-veneered plywood cabinet of similar size. The door of the old armoire was cracked open a few inches, and I could see that the cabinet was filled with long fluorescent light tubes and silver reflective Mylar. Violins hung from wires strung inside. These were light boxes, where Sam could speed along the natural aging and coloring and drying for which poor old Strad would have had to rely on low-tech sunlight. I thought back to that famous letter I'd looked at in the stultifying Museo di Stradivari in Cremona: "I beg you will forgive the delay with the violin, occasioned by the varnishing of the large cracks, that the sun may not re-open them." Sam did not depend solely on the sunlight of the Lombardy plain, nor did he have a sacred napping cot with a polar bear blanky so that he could take an afternoon siesta and impart his spirit into the drying violins. Considering the weight of tradition in his craft, these light boxes seemed a bold move toward modernity. Sam had to push his stool back to get the door open wide enough to let me into the varnish room. He got right to the point.

"I think I got the whole thing together on Friday," Sam told me. "Then I spent part of Saturday finishing the neck. I think I got it done done done in the white sometime on Saturday. Now it's in the light box. I washed it with a very light wash of pigment to seal it a little bit."

He opened the light box and pulled the Drucker fiddle down from where it hung. Sam held the violin out toward me, cradling the instrument like a baby, with one hand supporting the head of the scroll and another cupping the bottom. I'd seen a number of violins in the white around the shop. They were interesting and beautiful objects already, but there was a distinct blandness about them. An important character seemed to be missing. The violin, with just this early wash of pigment, had acquired a light cinnamon color, and a distinct shine. Sam rocked and turned the instrument.

"The wash put a texture right there in the channel," he said. "The ribs have a wave in them as well. And the spruce has a little bit of a corduroy texture now. Look at the scroll. Now you can see little tool marks."

He pointed to the twisting nautilus spirals cut into the wood, and sure enough, little stepped indentations were visible, giving evidence of how he'd worked his small wood chisel around the curve.

"These are not parts of the decoration," Sam said. "They're artifacts of the making process. I like to leave them. Some makers will sand them off or scrape them off. There's different styles. This is not intended to be a copy-copy of a specific instrument, but it's a Guarneri style, and I'm sort of letting myself go a little bit more in that direction. The scroll is a little more sculpted, and there's a little more tool marking than I might do on a Strad model. Lately I like to work that way better. It's a mix of highly finished surfaces and visible tool work.

"This is a cool moment to see a violin," Sam told me. "In fact, this is my favorite moment to see it. It goes from inanimate and quite dull—a nice matte and creamy—and then it's like when they turn the electricity on with Frankenstein. He jolts to life. With any luck this violin is going to wake up."

He stuck the violin back on the wire in the light box and turned back to the worktable. "I'm just going to get my brushes and tools together and start picking out the different sauces."

Before I'd left Cremona, while browsing in a bookstore dedicated to lutherie near the International Violin Making School, I'd found a little boxed paperback book called *Varnishes and Very Curious Secrets: Cremona 1747*. Even though it seemed absurdly expensive—forty euros—I bought it immediately. It turned out to be the translation of a text printed originally in Stradivari's hometown ten years after the master died, consisting of a series of recipes for varnishes for general use, like preparing paintings, or carved church pews, or, perhaps, finishing a violin. In an introduction to the original material, the book's twentieth-century editor, Vincenzo Gheroldi, describes a fact of eighteenth-century life of which I'd been completely unaware. People—for fun!—experimented with pigments and varnishes. The practice was a "cultural phenomenon," Gheroldi explains, that one priest of the day described as "virtuous entertainment."

How our notions of entertainment have changed. Maybe I'd gone a little native in the wilds of violin making, because it wasn't difficult for me to understand how, without television, someone would put away the dinner dishes, retire to the study, and mix up a batch of, say, a concoction called *bistre*. The recipe is as follows:

Refine as much as possible chimney soot, adding to it the urine of a child; put it into a glass, fill it with clear water, carefully mix using a stick, then let it rest. When most of the sediment has settled on the bottom, gently pour this liquid into another glass and let it rest for four days; what settles on the bottom of the glass is the best bistre. Repeat this procedure three times to remove sediment from any colour to be used on paper.

Somehow, I could easily imagine Stradivari doing that. I asked Sam if he mixed his own varnishes, without mentioning the use of the urine of a child.

"It used to be that if you wanted decent varnish you had to make it yourself," he said. "Now there are people who are making some very useable varnishes, which I've used occasionally, at least as a subingredient. I still cook my own. It's kind of like making a caramel." Sam was reaching around the table, pushing aside glass jars with different-colored stuff inside. Some of the jars had labels on them with dates.

"There's different batches here made at different times with slightly different ingredients," he said. "I'm not even sure where the chart is that is the key to what they are, so I don't know anymore what the exact ingredients are. But it hasn't varied much. Basically, the base of it is stuff that comes out of pine trees. That's what they make turpentine from. That's what they make rosin from. Between those two products you can make a lot of things."

He picked up one jar with "93" written on it, then picked up another unmarked jar. Both held viscous stuff that looked a little like maple syrup. "These are from the same batch, but one was cooked for quite a while. One I call 'medium' and you can see that the one cooked longer is darker." He held the jars up toward the weak gray light coming through the windows. "Even though the stuff is thick," Sam said, "it's still very transparent, very clear, very glow-ey."

So, I asked Sam, is this the kind of varnish that all vio-lin makers use? It turned out that what I was about to see was one of three steps in the *varnishing process*. What lay-men thought of as the varnish on a violin actually con-sisted of a first coat that soaked into the wood, called the ground; a second layer of something that was impervi-ous; then coats of actual varnish.

When Sam realized that, like most people, I was not aware of the stages of the process, he put the jars down and was quiet for a moment, like he was collecting his thoughts.

"We have to back up and go through the whole subject of ground," he began. "The ground is the most disputed and, I think, the most critical aspect, both for appearance and sound. I've done a few things to the wood already in terms of getting a patina on it. There's a little bit of natural oxidation on the surface. I washed on a little bit of natural pigment to get a little bit of color going. Now the fiddle is more or less like a prepared canvas. What-ever it is that goes on there first is what gets absorbed into the wood. So you kind of have one main go at getting it right." I could tell that this was another of those times where I was going to speak little and listen a lot.

"The first thing to understand," Sam continued, "is that if there is something to this whole mystery of the varnish thing, actually a lot of old fiddles—Strads as well as Guarneris and lots of others—have virtually none—*none*—of what we would normally call varnish left on them. Very, very often on old violins the varnish is just *gone*. It's been worn off and thinned down.

"So, if the *varnish proper* had that much to do with the sound you would say that a more worn violin wouldn't sound as good because it doesn't have that much varnish. But that's not the case. Even when the varnish wears off, what you would think you'd be looking at is bare wood. But what you're looking at has quite a lot of depth and fire visually—and color. So there's something on there that has penetrated the wood and doesn't come off easily.

"That's really the main thing I know about the ground. It penetrates into the wood. There's a quality that good instruments have, of having a shine when you turn the instrument in the light. The wood is reflective and also very refractive. When it works really well you can look through the wood almost like you've got a magnifying glass and it's like there's a lightbulb inside of it. That's a look I like."

Sam reached across his table and grabbed a jar full of an amber, waxy-looking stuff. He twisted off the lid and pushed it toward my nose. I sniffed, and it smelled a little flowery.

"Isn't that nice?" he asked. "That's propylis. It's something bees use to seal the hive. When beekeepers clean the hive they throw it away. Sacconi popularized it. I used to use it. You'd get this crud and soak it in alcohol, and a lot of wax and crap sinks to the bottom and you decant off this very pure material. It is a lovely color. It made a lovely ground. But it's actually very slow drying and I don't think it ever gets really crisp. So I don't use it anymore.

"Now, in Germany, in Mittenwald, they put pure linseed oil on the whole instrument and soak it on—quite a lot! And then you're supposed to let the instrument hang, for like a year, supposedly, is what they recommend. It's gorgeous, a very lovely finish. And it's very protected.

"But one of the characteristics of linseed oil is that it dries kind of leathery. So from the point of view of use it's good—you could sweat on the violin directly without hurting anything—but in terms of improving the vibration it actually does the opposite. It muffles things. The fiddle might sound very sweet, but it would lack a little of that sizzle."

Sam kept talking as he reached back into the light box to retrieve the Drucker fiddle. He talked of his mentor René Morel, who told Sam tales of his early days in America, working under Sacconi in the restoration and repair shop at the famous House of Wurlitzer shop on Forty-second Street in Manhattan, and how the other craftsmen there would hide their varnishes at night to keep their coworkers from discovering any secrets. During Sam's time with the Frenchman, he and Morel discussed varnishing a lot. Morel would talk about the best character of a ground and what it should do. He had cooked up what he considered a perfect "sauce." And there the sharing stopped. Morel refused to tell Sam exactly what was in it.

"I do believe what I'm doing here was inspired by René," Sam said as he reached around the table for his own sauce, pushing jars back and forth with increasing frustration. Finally, he found it. "Here it was right in front of me the whole time," he said, picking up a jar. I chose that moment to interrupt his disquisition and ask what was in the sauce. And in keeping with Morel's

tradition—what by now was a centuries-old tradition—
Sam refused to tell me.

I felt I didn't need to remind him that he'd written an
article for the trade magazine called *Strings* in which he
had described attending a gathering of violin makers in
Puerto Rico that was dedicated to the idea of sharing varnishing "secrets," and creating a new world where, as
Sam wrote, the "closed door atmosphere is starting to
yield." For a few minutes I tried gently to get the closed-
door atmosphere in our little closed-door room to yield,
to no avail.

"It's just one of those things," Sam said finally, letting
me know that the discussion would go no further. "A
good magician never tells all his tricks."

I can report this: the jar of sauce he used was labeled 13B
MEDIUM DARK.

Sam rubbed 13B Medium Dark onto the unfinished
Drucker violin with a cloth, at first using very light
strokes and putting on just a fine layer of color.

"This wood is quite interesting," he said at one point. "It
was soft when I was working with it and I was worried I
could overstain it. But that's not happening at all. I could
whack this thing even harder. It's not particularly absor-
bent." Eventually he switched to using a brush. It was a
small brush with short dark bristles made from the hair
of a squirrel. It looked as if it had seen a lot of fiddles.

"I've had this for about twenty years," Sam said.
"Which shows you how cheap I am."

Soon he cast aside the squirrel-hair brush and started
smearing 13B Medium Dark onto the fiddle with his

fingers. "I'm not sure OSHA would approve of my material-handling techniques," he told me, "but I'm a ravening beast when I varnish." He switched on the architect's lamp, revealing that it contained not a normal lightbulb but a heat lamp. It quickly got so hot being near it that I had to move my stool back from the worktable. Sam put on a big pair of tinted safety glasses that looked as if OSHA would approve. He moved in closer to the lamp.

"I'm kind of melting it into the violin," he said. "This needs to happen with time, but you can get a little head start with this lamp. I'm almost cooking it in, really impregnating the wood." As he worked, little wisps of smoke floated out of the violin through the f-holes. I wondered if he'd ever had a fiddle burst into flames but didn't think it was the proper time to ask.

I did ask Sam if he ever changed the nature or substance of what he used for the ground coat to try to achieve some different kind of sound from one of his violins. He kept stroking on "varnish" with his now completely stained fingers.

"This particular operation I don't vary much," he said. "I don't know if it's true, but I started using this sauce and I have a belief that this in part has something to do with the tone that I achieve with my instruments and I'm kind of scared to change it.

"I think I've tried to convey this to you in a lot of different ways," he continued. "But one doesn't always know why something works, and it's spooky. You keep asking yourself, *Shouldn't I know?* But you don't know *which* ingredient is the active ingredient in all this. And without extensive testing of every little aspect on and on and on,

keeping all other factors the same—which never happens—
you never really do know.

"So, I have a feeling for the way these instruments tend
to vibrate. When I apply this ground I can squeeze the instrument, and there's this little snap-crackle-pop. It just
sounds crisp.

"This material that I'm using, I feel like it just crawls
into the wood and becomes one with the wood. This
spruce was so soft and powdery when I worked on it—
this ground is going to glue all those fibers together. It's
not glue per se, but it'll have that effect. It's going to make
the surface of the wood feel stronger, and hopefully that
will make the material even more responsive to the tiny
little vibrations. It'll have more of that sizzle-y kind of
vibration when it's played, which gives a more complex,
shaped sound."

Sam stopped rubbing ground into the violin, wiped
his hands on a rag and on his apron. A little over an
hour had passed since he'd started, and sure enough,
the fiddle had awakened, Frankenstein-like. There
was a life and character to it. The surface was still a little wet, and as Sam cradled it in his hands again and rocked
it back and forth the light bounced off its various surfaces,
making the flamed maple of the back seem almost three-
dimensional, showing a depth and texture in the parallel
grain of the spruce belly. Sam hung the Drucker violin
back in the light box.

"All right," he said. "Now you have gone where few
have gone before you."

I felt both privileged and stymied. Going *anywhere* in

this topsy-turvy world of violin making seemed so often like going down the proverbial rabbit hole. It wasn't any different with "varnish." Today I had learned that in this important process, as with so many other parts of building a fiddle, the real secret was that there was no secret. I was getting accustomed to that revelation. Yes, these varnish secrets were very curious indeed. All along *this* secret had been hiding in plain sight. What people had for centuries thought of as varnish was really just a kind of makeup that covered the skin underneath. And the important part of the beauty of a violin, both in sight and sound, really was skin deep, in the pores of the wood.

I would go home that night and reread Sir James Beament's chapter on varnish in *The Violin Explained*. He had become my clear-eyed, no-nonsense go-to guy. Beament's analysis of varnish went all the way down to the chemical level, describing chains of carbon, hydrogen, and oxygen molecules. But I always returned to the Cambridge don for a knowing, skeptical global view.

The classical makers of Cremona, Beament wrote, "can have known no more about why varnish worked than why their wooden boxes did." Varnish, Beament concluded, since it was the most cosmetic part of a fiddle, had provoked a phenomenon that is still being used by the cosmetics industry—convincing people that there must be a secret ingredient that enhanced physical beauty, or, in the case of the violin, created a beautiful sound.

Before I left Sam's shop that day, we talked about the end run toward finishing the Drucker fiddle. With the ground on, he would leave it in the light box to dry for a week or more. Then he would apply several layers of what he had called *varnish proper*, maybe three or four coats total. They would also need to dry. Then he'd go over the brand-new fiddle to make it look like it was a few hundred years old. Gene Drucker had ordered—and was willing to pay extra for—an "antiqued" violin. In the top echelons of the classical music world, no fiddle player wanted an instrument that looked new, even if a top living maker crafted it. Such was the strength of the cult of old age.

"If I finish the varnishing and get it dry by Mother's Day," Sam said, "I'm prepared to be gonzo about it and do a marathon antiquing session. Really go at it. I could have the fiddle ready for Gene by his birthday party. It's doable."

Chapter 12

DELIVERY

He did it.

The next time I went to Brooklyn, as I trudged up the now-familiar four flights of stairs to Sam's shop, I could hear the sound of a violin—beautifully played—get louder and louder. On the top landing, I stood behind the door for a moment before walking in, listening to a passage from one of the Bach partitas. I'd heard Sam test violins many times, and though he is a very competent fiddler, it certainly was not him playing. The music stopped and a voice inside said, "Wow. Wow! That's really great." I went in.

Sam was leaning against the baby grand piano, where two violins rested on their backs. Wiltrud was perched on the arm of one of the worn sofas. In the middle of the room stood a neatly but casually dressed middle-aged Asian man, a violin in his hand. This was Cho-Liang Lin, whom nearly everyone calls Jimmy. He is one of the top violin soloists in the world. *Strings* magazine described him as a "splendid Taiwan-born virtuoso, renowned for his soulful expression of emotion in classic, romantic, and modern music." Like Gene Drucker, he was trained at Juilliard, where he worked with Dorothy DeLay, one of the most famous and respected violin teachers of this century.

Early in his career, Lin had played on several Stradivari instruments. None of them completely satisfied his needs. Then, as he told *Strings*, "I saw the 1734 'Duc de Camposelice' Guarneri 'del Gesù' in the Charles Beare shop in London and fell in love with it." He managed to buy it. But the violinist was not so in love with his del Gesù that he didn't realize that it, like many old fiddles, was prone to getting out of sorts when subjected to the demands of quick international travel. I had met Lin in Sam's shop once before, and he'd told me of going from a concert in frigid and snowy Montreal to another in hot, humid San Antonio. After nursing his 250-year-old fiddle through the harsh changes, Lin decided to commission a modern instrument from Sam, and he began to entrust Sam with maintenance of his del Gesù.

Sam had told *Strings*, "As a person he's extremely gracious—when you meet him, you feel he's an almost natural aristocrat, with an old-fashioned graciousness. The new violin he's commissioned from me was designed in terms of his playing style, the personal way a player has of drawing out sound from a string. I don't rely on recordings for that kind of thing. When he comes to my studio, he plays for me. I wouldn't rely on electronic equipment for that."

Today, Jimmy Lin was in Brooklyn to pick up his Guarneri, which had been in the shop for some maintenance. Sam took the opportunity to have him test the just-finished Drucker fiddle. It was just a few days before Gene's birthday party, where the violin would be ceremoniously delivered.

The Drucker violin looked quite different from the last time I'd seen it, when Sam finished his brush-and-fingertip application of the ground coat and stuck it into the light box to dry. Before applying the "varnish proper," he'd put on a coat of amber, which is a very tough resin. The purpose was to create what he called an "isolating layer" on the fiddle, so that subsequent coats of varnish could not impregnate the pores of the wood.

Then, Sam reported, "I used an oil varnish with a resin component, and cooked it to make it dryer and more colorful." The color was an orange-brown, with more of the golden brown color coming through. "I figured that would look nice," Sam said.

As he applied the varnish proper, Sam simultaneously started to "antique" the instrument, trying to make the brand-new fiddle appear to have hundreds of years of use and wear. It is not as controversial as the tension in a bass-bar, but luthiers argue over the propriety of antiquing a new violin. Some violin makers refuse to antique a new instrument, arguing that, at the least, it perpetuates the cult of old age that permeates their world; some go as far as to say it is dishonest to make a new instrument look old.

Sam Zygmuntowicz is a very practical craftsman who realizes that his clients want instruments that appear old, and in the tradition of his father, the laundryman, he gives customers what they want. Besides, he told me, the antiqued instrument had more character and was more interesting to look at than a pristine, perfectly varnished new instrument. "Once you've worked with old fiddles," Sam said, "it's hard to get used to working with new, straight varnish. One of the things that makes old instruments look so interesting is the few little nicks and the added contrast."

To achieve the result of making new look old, Sam developed a technique of taking the pristine fiddle and giving it decades worth of wear in a day—sort of like time-lapse photography.

"To the extent possible," he told me, "I try to emulate the real wear that happens. While I'm varnishing it I start to wear it in realistic ways—hand abrasion, thumbnail chips, scratches, a lot of handling. Then I'll put a film over it, a light wash of rosin that has a yellow, brown, and gray in it naturally.

"I'll add a little lampblack from a candle to that, a very thin wash that you're almost not aware of. I used to just burn a candle on a hot plate and dip my brush in it. Because that's where a lot of contrast in the old fiddles actually came from: being in houses lit by lamps and candles and heated with fireplaces. Soot was in the air."

Now, in the studio, Jimmy Lin held the Drucker fiddle

against his neck and played a bit of a violin concerto. I could recognize the melody but couldn't name it offhand. He put down the Drucker and picked up his Guarneri and played the same passage.

"I don't know," Lin said.

"Which one was that?" Wiltrud asked.

"It was the Guarneri," Sam told her.

"Does it sound like it's worth four million dollars more?" Jimmy Lin asked.

Nobody in the room dared to answer the question.

A few days later, I snuck into the upstairs club called Fez at a restaurant called Time Café on Broadway on the Upper West Side. Gene Drucker's wife, Roberta, had planned a surprise party for her husband's fiftieth birthday, and I knew that if Gene saw me, he'd really know something was up. The room was already crowded with people, and I recognized the other three players from the Emerson, and Sam and his wife, Liza, over in the corner.

Gene arrived with Roberta a few moments later and seemed genuinely surprised. There was singing and applause and congratulations. And then Sam stood up and called for the room to hush. He walked with a violin case to the front of the room, near the bar, opened the case, and pulled out the new violin. Later, he would tell me that he was very nervous preparing to play a violin solo in front of a big group of top-level classical musicians.

Sam tucked the violin under his chin, raised the bow, and performed a fiddle tune called "West Virginia Gals." He received warm applause from the crowd while Gene strode to where Sam stood and received the fiddle. He turned the fiddle around to see it himself and show it to the crowd. He played a few short passages and then put it back in the case. Through the rest of the party many of his friends would take a chance at playing the new instrument. In fact, the violin moved around the room like a brilliant and attractive party guest, and every time I looked there was a small knot of people around it, giving the fiddle their undivided attention.

Now the Drucker violin belonged to Drucker. Nobody, least of all the violinist or the violin maker, knew how he would react to it. As I was leaving the party, I stopped to look at the new fiddle one last time. It was momentarily alone, lying on a table near the door, and even in the murky light of the nightclub it was beautiful; its glowing brown varnish had a patina of age, and when I rocked it a bit, the light hit on the facets of tool work that Sam had left on the carved spiral of the scroll. How I wished I could pick up this violin and throw off a passage from the Bach partitas. I'd spent so many hours with the pieces of wood that made up this finished fiddle. Silly as it seemed, I couldn't help feeling a pang of regret and nostalgia, now that it was finished, as if it were a child going off to college.

The case sat nearby, and it was then that I noticed Sam had made a bumper sticker and stuck it onto the side. It read: MY *OTHER* FIDDLE IS A STRAD.

Chapter 13

WHAT YOU HEAR
UNDER YOUR EAR

fter the birthday party I started playing the new violin," Gene Drucker told me later. "I was working on a Mozart concerto that I was going to play that summer at a festival in upstate New York.

"I liked the openness of the sound. My wife, Roberta, found it very big. But something started happening. The sound was so direct, so penetrating, that it was almost too much under my ear, without as much sweetness leavening the punch and the volume as I might desire.

"About a week after that we went to Vienna. The quartet was doing that theater piece based on Shostakovich—*The Noise of Time*. Written by the British playwright Simon McBurney, *The Noise of Time* is a multimedia performance that examines the Russian composer's life and work from the Nazi siege of Leningrad to his complicated and controversial connection with Stalin and later Communist regimes. The Emerson Quartet is used to great effect. The musicians mix onstage with actors, and live music mixes with recorded sound and visual effects. Ultimately, the musicians play Shostakovich's haunting and powerful fifteenth string quartet, his last, which many think he wrote as his own requiem.

"I used the new violin for that performance in Vienna," Drucker said. "It worked fine for that. And I kept preparing the Mozart concerto and was also working on a Bartók sonata and some other repertoire for the summer festival. I remember practicing in that hotel room in Vienna and liking some things about the new fiddle and not being totally convinced about other things and wondering, What I define as quality in my innermost set of definitions as a violinist—Does this violin really have it, or not?"

When next I talked to Sam Zygmuntowicz after the birthday party, I asked him what he knew about Gene's reaction to the new violin. "For Gene," he told me, "he's surprisingly all right with the whole thing.

"For Gene," he added.

Sam talked for a while about his theory of psychoacoustics, and the important interface between the player and the instrument. "Strads have a way they like to be played," he said. "Gene will have to adapt to the new fiddle. This is a Guarneri model and is a little different and you've got to play it that way. He's got a fiddle now that will allow him to whack it. It will be able to bring out other aspects of his playing."

Drucker had visited Sam's shop for what the violin maker described as part sound post adjustment, part pep talk. "He played all kinds of music while he was here," Sam reported. "Excerpts from the quartet repertoire, concertos. He really played extended passages and it was very emotional. Sometimes I had to interrupt him. He just wants to crawl into the music."

I wanted to go with Sam to see Gene give one of the first public performances on the new fiddle. Vienna was a little beyond our means, and the quartet was leaving town again for its annual stint at the Aspen Music Festival in Colorado, where Gene had so much trouble with his Strad years before while recording the Shostakovich quartets. That also seemed too long a haul. So Sam and I agreed to get together for a mid-July concert by the Emerson Quartet at the Caramoor Music Festival, a prestigious summer series presented on the grounds of a former estate about an hour north of New York City.

The day of the concert was one of those humid northeast summer days where you feel you've been wrapped in a hot wet blanket. Sam and I had driven from completely different directions to be there, and met near the ticket booth. "Well," the violin maker said, "this is quite a change from Brooklyn." The site was gorgeous, green and lush, bordered by old dry-laid stone walls, and dotted with prim, carefully tended gardens. The crowd milling around us was a typical classical music audience, well turned out and mostly older. We found our seats just before the quartet took the stage.

The Emerson has long been notable in its world for the uncommon practice where the two violinists alternate playing the first and second parts. In most quartets, one violinist always takes the lead; Drucker and Setzer act as equals. On the three pieces scheduled for this day's program, Gene would only play first fiddle on one, a Beethoven quartet. He played all his parts with his usual intensity, both emotional and precise. He blended well when that was required, and soared above the other players a few times when the music called for it. I had been to a number of Emerson concerts by then and had listened to the group's recordings a lot. To my ear, on this new violin, Drucker sounded like Drucker. I kept sneaking glances at Sam throughout the concert, trying to get a sense of his reaction. He listened studiously, with his chin cupped in his hand. At the end of the program there were the usual ovations.

"What did you think of the fiddle?" I asked Sam.

"Very good," he said. "I'm quite happy with the way it sounded today. I hope Gene is too." We headed toward a fenced area that served as an outdoor artists' greenroom.

There was a knot of friends and well-wishers of the Emerson in the little enclave, but Sam became the center of attention as soon as he entered. All of the quartet members, led by the exuberant cellist David Finckel, hugged the violin maker and praised his new fiddle effusively. Even Drucker, the least demonstrative of the four, seemed to beam. His wife, Roberta, was there, and at one point she said, "Now Gene can sell his Strad and we'll be in much, much better financial shape." Everyone laughed. I'm almost certain she was joking.

I kept in touch with Gene throughout the next weeks of the summer. I wanted to hear him play the new violin again and hoped it might be out of his normal context in the quartet. It was nearing August when he was scheduled to play that Mozart concerto he'd been practicing in Vienna. He would appear as a soloist with a small orchestra at a music festival on one of the Finger Lakes in Skaneateles, New York. That seemed like a perfect opportunity, and I blocked out a few days to drive there for the concert.

I got a phone call the day before I was to leave. It was Gene on a cell phone—the reception was so spotty that he seemed to be yelling to me from the bottom of a well. "I'm very glad I caught you before you left," he said. "I just wanted to tell you that I may not be playing the new violin tomorrow, and I wouldn't want you to drive all the way up here for nothing."

"What's wrong?" I asked him.

"I'm just not sure if using Sam's violin would be the right thing," he told me. "I've been going back and forth between it and my Strad, and I'm thinking now that I would feel better using the Strad. I guess I can say that I'll almost definitely use the Strad."

"I'm sorry to hear that," I said to Gene. "But of course I understand. I hope you don't mind if I don't come up."

"No, no," he said, "that's fine. I hope there'll be another opportunity soon." He paused for a moment, and I heard nothing but the hollow muted static of the cell phone. Then Gene said, "Using this new violin is making me reconsider entirely what my sound could be." He didn't seem excited by this new violin playing experience, as he had written Sam a few months before. The violinist sounded like he was in pain.

Later, when I asked Gene what was going on in his mind during those days in upstate New York, he told me: "I guess I called you the day before the concert, because I knew you needed to know. But even up to the last minute on the day of the performance I was going back and forth. I couldn't decide. After the last rehearsal, with only a few hours left before the performance, I stayed behind and was still going back and forth between the two instruments. Finally, I did use the Strad."

Not only was Drucker hearing something quite different under his ear with Sam's fiddle than he did with the Strad, but he was also feeling something different too. "There's much more tension in the strings," he told me. "Under my right hand [which holds the bow] I would have expected it. What surprised me was that under my left hand it made my fingers hurt, even when I used exactly the same kind of strings. That difference physically is part of the whole package.... That's why it's easier to play stuff [on the new violin] that has to be loud and forceful and where the response has to be very fast. That's why it's more difficult for me to feel that I can *mold* the sound in the most lyrical phrases, especially in earlier music."

Violinists know that a new fiddle requires some breaking in—they call it "playing in." How long that takes varies with each instrument, and the more extreme theorists say it requires decades of playing for a violin to fully mature. During the initial break-in period for the Drucker violin, whenever I talked with Sam Zygmuntowicz, I commiserated with him. It seemed that the worst-case scenario was being played out, and that this fiddle was making Gene feel uncomfortable. But the violin maker was mostly stoic. He kept insisting that he would work with Gene to make everything right. "Pleasing finicky people is one of the useful skills for being able to ply your art," he told me. But Sam was worried most that Drucker would not want to take the trouble to go through the process of making the new instrument right. "If Gene gets discouraged early," Sam said, "it's going to be very difficult to get him undiscouraged."

About four months after the Drucker violin became Gene's fiddle, I stopped into an Emerson Quartet rehearsal at cellist David Finckel's apartment in Manhattan, and joined the group for a lunch break at a nearby restaurant. Throughout the meal, the musicians talked about the importance of sound, yet how variable it was between instruments and the people playing them. "Every person who plays makes a different sound," violinist Phil Setzer said. "So even if you had the same instrument and ten different people play on it, it would sound different. It's really true with fiddles, but it's even true with pianos, and that's putting your fingers down on a mechanical contraption, in a way." Setzer and his colleagues had recently attended a memorial service for Isaac Stern, where three different world-class pianists played music on the same piano.

"Each sounded beautiful," Setzer said, "but it sounded like they wheeled out different pianos for each one."

As the talk continued, going through the inevitable comparisons between new instruments and those built by the old guys, we seemed to be getting dangerously close to the precipice of that void called What Do We Really Know? Drucker, who hadn't been talking much, took over the conversation.

"I think I've said this to you before," he told me. "Phil and David took to their new instruments from Sam immediately. But neither one of them had a Strad. They both had very fine instruments, but I have to say that no matter how much trouble I sometimes have with my Strad and the kind of up-and-down relationship I have with it—it's still one of the best early Strads, and Stradivari is still the greatest violin maker who ever lived. So it's harder to just say, 'Okay, I don't need that anymore.' The soul nourishment that my Strad has given me when it's in good shape, the sort of aura of the sound is something that ..." He paused for a moment. None of the other musicians broke in. I had heard from Sam that the other players in the Emerson liked the new violin and thought Gene should play it instead of the Stradivari. Finally, Gene said, "Well, we'll see how things develop."

Early the next year, Sam took the Drucker violin back to his workbench, pulled it apart, and regraduated some thicknesses on the back and belly, particularly around the edges. He worked a bit on the bass-bar, too. The ultimate effect he was hoping to achieve was to make the fiddle more flexible, which would help make it feel more like Gene's Stradivari. While building the new violin Sam had left the wood a little thick because the old wood he was using seemed so light to him. It was one of those cases where, all things being equal, nothing was ever equal. "I was a little too conservative," he realized.

Drucker got his new violin back and returned to trying to fit it into his musical life. "I wish I could have just adopted it," he told me later, "but I just couldn't." Several times, the new fiddle got a good chance to win him over. The Emerson was engaged in a fairly unusual recording of Johann Sebastian Bach's famous *Art of the Fugue*. It was music that was not originally written for strings, and when the players hashed out their interpretation, Drucker thought the new violin might work better, and he used it for the recording, which became the Emerson's best-selling album.

"For this Bach, somehow, the problems I was having playing the new violin didn't matter as much," Gene said. "First of all, the recording started at a point where I was most frustrated with the Strad. And that particular Bach is more austere and less personal sounding than much of the music we play—certainly less personal than the Bach sonatas and partitas. I don't mean to say the music is merely academic. It's not, and we were trying to get to a deeper level of meaning in that music. But it was fine for me to be using the new instrument on that. It was open and healthy sounding."

Still, Drucker remained steadfast to his Stradivari, most of the time. He just couldn't completely warm to the sound of the Zygmuntowicz in that most intimate setting, cradled between his shoulder and his left ear.

"What I've noticed as the difference in quality that I hear under my ear," Gene told me later, "is that it just seems to me the Strad has a more beautiful, more refined sound. I really think that's true. The difference is greater under my ear than even on a recording. When I hear it played back, the Zygmuntowicz sounds rounder and sweeter than I think it sounds as I'm playing it. And I suppose in a concert hall there's even more difference. Something that I perceive under my ear as being on the harsh side may not necessarily be perceived that way at a distance.

"It's that instrument," he concluded, sounding more than a little weary with the whole subject, "but it's also me and my personality quirks."

The violinist would continue to wrestle with his choice for months, bringing to the struggle not only those personality quirks, but also his substantial talent, high-level training, and long experience. He'd spent two decades playing some of the best music ever written on an instrument made by one of the supreme craftsmen of all time. While he was willing to entertain the possibility that he was some sort of follower in the Stradivari cult, in the end, Drucker knew he had to trust what he heard under his ear.

"You learn about yourself over time," he told me. "And I think this whole experience convinced me that I may just be a Strad player after all."

In his workshop in Brooklyn, Sam Zygmuntowicz came to accept that with this one fiddle he'd lost the contest for a violinist's soul. "Gene's really tried to take to my violin. But it's like a demon that he wrestles with. He hasn't fallen in love with it."

Sam did what craftsmen do—went back to work. He had years' worth of commissions to fulfill, and when he sat at his workbench, each day was another step in trying to better understand the complicated dynamics of those magical wooden boxes he built. He was coming to believe that the best innovation in his trade might simply be a fuller and more clear-sighted understanding of the tradition he'd inherited.

"Not all Strads are great, but there really is something to these old fiddles," Sam said. "Violinists on Gene's level have the most highly calibrated ears and hands on earth, and there's a consensus feeling that there's *something* in there. And you're really not going to go forward by denying it.

"There are very, very subtle differences between a Strad and ordinary violins."

Not many people in the business think Sam Zygmuntowicz makes merely ordinary violins. He might be as close as any living luthier to understanding what those subtle differences are and, most importantly, making them disappear. So he keeps working, long removed from those days when some guys in a little town in Lombardy had gotten things awfully right. Here it is, the twenty-first century, Brooklyn, and with every measurement he makes, every cut and scrape, the old guy looms over his shoulder.

In the end, the violin maker told me, "Stradivari and I have a complicated and intimate relationship. I'm willing to yield ground—somewhat graciously—to Strad. For now."

Chapter 14

CODA

In the fall of 2003 and spring of 2004, as it neared two years since Gene had received his new violin, the Emerson Quartet descended into an ornate theater at the American Academy of Arts and Letters in the upper reaches of Manhattan to record the music of Felix Mendelssohn. It was another of the comprehensive and definitive projects for which the quartet had become known, for it would include all seven of the nineteenth-century German prodigy's full string quartets, a few shorter pieces for four fiddles, and, as a bonus, the well-known Octet, masterfully written by Mendelssohn when he was just sixteen years old.

Naturally, there was a question of how the Emerson

Quartet would go about recording the Mendelssohn *Octet*. In an unusual twist, the group decided to perform all eight parts themselves, using the technique called over tracking, where parts are recorded separately and then combined onto the final finished track. The technique is quite common in popular music but virtually unheard of, and somewhat frowned upon, in classical music recording. To add more spin, the Emerson chose to use four old Italian instruments for half of the parts and four Sam Zygmuntowicz instruments for the other half. Since the Zygmuntowicz Drucker fiddle had come into the quartet, violist Larry Dutton had been won over and commissioned Sam to build him a new instrument, an altered version of his 1796 viola built by the Milanese maker named Pietro Giovanni Mantegazza.

Considering their track record, few would question the musical seriousness of the Emerson, though some critics would call the Octet concept something of a stunt. When I heard about the project it seemed to me a playful volley in the continuing game of comparing old instruments to new. The musicians vowed to never reveal publicly which parts were played on which instruments. Would listeners be able to tell?

All of this "seemed like a wild yet intriguing idea," Gene Drucker would write in liner notes published with the recording, which would win the group another Grammy. As the quartet was nearing completion of the Octet recording, Gene invited me to come and watch a session.

Whatever wildness had originally struck the musicians when they'd had this idea, by that point they had settled into a more mundane workaday professionalism. The record label had commissioned a video to be made of the Octet recording, and as I watched it later, the players seem downright giddy with excitement as they listen to playbacks of the Emerson Quartet playing with the Emerson Quartet. On the day I visited they were doing touch-ups of shorter sections, and the breaks to hear playbacks were brief and to the point. During a longer break for lunch, no one mentioned music at all; the talk centered on travel arrangements for an upcoming tour and future bookings.

When the musicians went back to work after lunch, settling into chairs on the microphone-cluttered stage of the theater, I sat in a backstage chamber with their producer and recording engineer, Da-Hong Seetoo, in front of a bank of computers that he had built himself and a large monitor and keyboard that served as his control panel. He'd win a Grammy Award for this project, too. Da-Hong, who studied at Juilliard and is an excellent violinist, handed me a musical score covered with highlighted passages, designating the parts that each musician would play.

In a live performance, each player would stay on one part for the duration—second violin, say. But for these special recording conditions, the Emerson had deconstructed the Octet, and parts were mixed and matched for each "take" of the recording to make the music flow better.

When Da-Hong would punch the "record" button and the live quartet would join the four instruments already recorded, the sound in the control room was full and solid and wonderfully exciting. I followed the score closely. Try as I might, I could not even guess which instrument was being used, a Zygmuntowicz or a Cremonese masterwork. Later, Gene all but verified for me which instrument he'd used for the first violin part. I won't reveal the secret, but I can say that though I have listened to the recording dozens of times, I still can't tell the difference.

This just seemed to accentuate some misgivings I was having at this time. As I tried to make sense of my long journey exploring the world of violins, I had to play a variation of the game Sam Zygmuntowicz liked to start with his colleagues in Oberlin; I had to ask myself, *"What have I really learned?"*

My first answer was always, "What a strange world it is."

I suppose that's what happens to anyone who tries to understand magic. Once its techniques are known and observed a lot of the magic goes away. After all the hours I'd spent watching Sam cut and carve the Drucker fiddle, and now, hearing it played marvelously alongside a Stradivari and a Guarneri del Gesù that was being used by Phil Setzer, I could appreciate why the old guys' violins were so revered: they sounded great. But so did the new Zygmuntowicz. At least to my ears.

During one break in the recording session, I was sitting in the control room chatting with Phil Setzer. While he talked, he absentmindedly cradled and stroked the violin he was playing that day.

Because he used his Zygmuntowicz violin almost exclusively, Setzer had to borrow an old fiddle for this project, and he'd been able to use one belonging to David Fulton, who is a computer software millionaire and in recent years has amassed one of the best collections of violins in the world, many of which he lends to top performers. Fulton had lent Setzer the favorite fiddle of the late Isaac Stern, the 1737 Guarneri del Gesù known as the Panette.

There we were, sitting on folding chairs in a rather dingy basement room. Setzer pushed the fiddle in my direction and asked, "Have you ever held anything worth five million dollars?" He let my fingers grasp the del Gesù for a brief moment and then pulled the violin back with a comic flourish. I have listened to the sections of the finished Octet recording where I know Setzer is using the del Gesù, and, once again, I cannot pinpoint a real difference, let alone a $4.975 million difference.

I understood Sam's position that it was futile to keep questioning whether the old instruments really were better—accept the fact and keep working. But in the final analysis of what I'd learned about new fiddles and old fiddles and the violinists who played them, I once again found that Sir James Beament seemed to get it right. In the last chapter of *The Violin Explained* he concluded that it was simply the prime market force of supply and demand that determined the astronomical prices paid for the famous old guys' violins. However, Beament wrote, "They do not make any different sound, and no audience can tell what instrument is being played. But if a player thinks he plays better on such an instrument, he will." And, "audiences are even more susceptible to suggestion than players." That's not going to change anytime soon.

In the year after he finished the violin for Gene Drucker, Sam went on filling his various commissions. Then, in May of 2003, the estate of Isaac Stern put up for sale the two del Gesù copies Sam had built for the Maestro. The sale was handled by a new online auction house named for the great hunter of violins, Tarisio. Sam's copy of Stern's Panette sold for $130,000, which was a record price for an instrument crafted by a living violin maker.

In the weeks and months after that auction, Sam dealt nearly constantly with calls for new commissions. He raised his price for a new fiddle to more than $40,000. Despite that (or maybe because of that), his waiting list just kept getting longer. Soon, it would include two of the most heralded strings players of our time. One was superstar violinist Joshua Bell, who played on a Stradivari known as the Gibson ex Huberman, a fiddle whose history was picaresque, and included going missing for decades after being stolen from backstage at Carnegie Hall. The other was Yo-Yo Ma, who has lifetime possession (on loan from an anonymous owner) of one of the most revered instruments in the world, the cello known as the Davidov. It had previously been used by Jacqueline du Pré.

"It happens that a number of my clients own Strads," Sam told me. "They're coming to me for something very specific. Unfortunately—though I'm not really complaining—that sets the bar a little higher."

Before finishing this book, I joined Sam for one last time in Oberlin. He'd stopped attending the workshop dedicated to violin making and had switched to a weeklong gathering of researchers in violin acoustics that included scientists and more technically minded violin makers. Sam said he felt he'd learned about as much as he could about building the box from his violin making colleagues; he was now most excited about understanding the science underlying how the boxes vibrated. "The key to innovation," he told me, "is more knowledge." But even the scientists were still trying to discover the "secrets" of Stradivari. Not long before this, a climatologist from Columbia University and a dendrochronologist from the University of Tennessee (one of the men who'd been part of the tree ring circus dispute over the authenticity of the Messiah) published a paper speculating that the wood Stradivari used in his violins was especially strong because it grew during a peculiar 70-year climatological period known as the Maunder Minimum, or "little Ice Age," when colder weather would have made trees grow slower and denser.

Nobody mentioned that discovery in the few days I spent sitting in on the acoustics workshops at Oberlin. Most of the information presented was rather opaque—PowerPoint presentations full of charts and equations. Luckily, like the violin makers I'd first met here in Ohio, the acoustics group held a friendly cocktail hour and dinner and then most people headed back to the workshop for more informal, at-ease evening sessions. I'd been in these workshop rooms before. It was the same building where on a hot night several years ago, a violin maker had introduced me to the notion of the magical box. This time, things were different. The centers of attention this night were acoustic testing machines that could record a spectrum of sound output from a fiddle that was carefully positioned before a microphone and tapped on the bridge with a little hammer. Compared to this, the violin making workshop had indeed seemed like a bunch of old Geppettos carving away. Now the rooms had the look and feel of a laboratory.

Late that night Sam took me to his workbench and showed me an instrument he'd created for testing. "Here's Gluey," he said, holding up the violin. It was a cheap factory-made fiddle that he'd taken apart, scraping the belly and back as thin as he would ever dare. He put in a bass-bar, gave the fiddle some varnish, and set up the strings and sound post for a professional player. Then he made a bunch of veneerlike patches in various sizes that he could stick on and pull off the belly and back as he wished. The purpose was to test how changing thicknesses in various places affected the vibration of the top and back plates and how that altered the sound. Though much of the experimentation was recorded the old-fashioned way—using unreliable ears—Sam also had built his own contraption, which measured the sound spectrum created by plucking one of the strings. The results are recorded by special acoustics software on his laptop computer.

Over the next few hours Sam talked and talked and tested and tested. Time seemed to stop for him, and I got more and more tired. He said things like: "We've gone from a static approach to a dynamic approach. Violins aren't static; they're changing all the time. Every part is moving." At one point he pulled out his laptop and showed me a three-dimensional "movie" of a violin vibrating, complete with air being pushed out of the f-holes.

"Isn't this cool?" Sam asked. "What's important is what's invisible, but I think technology will help us see the invisible."

Whether he was right, or whether he would ever realize his notions, or whether that will help him make fiddles better than those of the old guys, I don't know. But I finally understood then that I had been given a window into a room that few of us ever see in the modern world. What I'd witnessed in his workshop was craft; what I was seeing tonight seemed to be the true soul of craftsmanship. Sam was here, essentially, on vacation. He'd been in the workshops since early morning and it was approaching midnight. As the great sociologist C. Wright Mills wrote in his study of work in the book *White Collar*, "The craftsman's way of livelihood determines and infuses his entire mode of living…. There is no split of work and play." Not only was Sam Zygmuntowicz a very successful violin maker, but he was also a lucky guy.

I had been playing the trumpet a lot around this time, and one job I got was to perform in the backup band for a variety show. This was not your run-of-the-mill variety show but one produced, directed, and largely starring priests from the diocese of Scranton, my hometown, where I'd played at the funeral of the governor and heard the young violinist play Irving Berlin, and, for all intents, started on this whole project.

For this show, there was only one short and frighteningly disorganized rehearsal in the late afternoon before the first performance. In the run-through of one number, a priest with a very good voice sang Charlie Chaplin's song "Smile," accompanied by an accomplished pianist, who happened also to be a monsignor. After the first time through the lyrics they asked me to play a short solo but said I wouldn't have to play it during the actual show.

The night of the performance, a young violinist showed up to play that solo—the same young violinist who'd played "How Deep Is the Ocean" in church and spun a web of sound that enveloped hundreds of mourners and made them hold their breath. He wasn't quite so young now; he'd gone through a conservatory and was starting his career. He played beautifully, infusing Chaplin's song with more sophistication and an even richer sound than he'd achieved with Irving Berlin's tune. The odds were against him: the show was in a big, sterile auditorium, with such acts as a priest doing ethnic jokes and others lip-synching and dancing to the disco hit "YMCA," but once again, the violinist reached the heights of poignancy.

Backstage afterward, I introduced myself and told him how good he sounded. Naturally, I asked him what kind of fiddle he was playing. "It's about a hundred years old," the violinist said. "It belonged to my grandfather. It was made in Romania." He mentioned the maker's name, but I didn't recognize it.

As he wiped off the violin and placed it in the case, the violinist said to me, "I like to think that this fiddle has a gypsy soul."

After all I'd seen and heard in this strange and magical world of violins, I wasn't going to argue with him.

Source Notes

The bulk of what is presented here is based on many hours with Sam Zygmuntowicz in his workshop, taking notes, or, more often, running a tape recorder as he described what he was doing and the principles behind it. The result was hundreds of pages of transcripts from which I drew much of the narration. I did the same in my more limited time with Gene Drucker. In keeping with standard journalistic practice, neither Sam nor Gene was given any prior review or approval of the text.

I also drew from articles by Zygmuntowicz and about him in the main journals of the trade. They included various issues of *The Journal of the Violin Society of America*, *The Strad*, and *Strings*. Those three journals were also helpful in informing me about various other subjects in the book as well as giving me a continuing understanding of issues in the world of fiddles.

The first book that caught my attention was Edward Heron-Allen's *Violin-Making as it was, and is,* and I find myself returning to it often because it is so strange and charming. Sam Zygmuntowicz told me that when he reads Heron-Allen now, the eccentric Englishman seems even more astute.

James Beament's *The Violin Explained: Components, Mechanism and Sound* really became my "go-to" source. It is a tad technical, but Beament's scientific skepticism, combined with his intimacy with the subject—he plays the bass fiddle and is married to a violin maker—makes for a clear-eyed analysis of how violins, old and new, function on the player and listener.

The Hills' survey of Stradivari was invaluable. *Antonio Stradivari: His Life and Work (1644–1737)* has stayed in print so long for obvious reasons. I also used the Hills' subsequent *The Violin-Makers of the Guarneri Family (1626–1762)*. Simone Sacconi's *'Secrets' of Stradivari* is likewise indispensable for understanding Stradivari's work. And, for my purposes, it gave great insight into Sacconi himself. That understanding was buttressed by a collection of reminiscences of Sacconi published in 1985 by the Cremonese Association of Professional Violin Makers, titled, *From Violin Making to Music: The Life and Works of Simone Fernando Sacconi*.

A more circumscribed look at Stradivari's work—*Stradivari's Genius: Five Violins, One Cello, and Three Centuries of Enduring Perfection*—was written recently by Toby Faber and was quite helpful. An entertaining look at one Stradivari instrument and its restoration by Sam's former boss, René Morel, is Nicholas Delbanco's 2001 book *The Countess of Stanlein Restored: A History of the Countess of Stanlein Ex Pananini Stradivarius Cello of 1707*.

Several more general looks at the violin and its world were very helpful. The most readable is one from the early 1970s by Joseph Wechsberg called *The Glory of the Violin*. More academic in tone, but no less helpful, were Alberto Bachmann's *An Encyclopedia of the Violin*, first published in 1925, but still available; and *The Violin Family* (various authors) from the New Grove Musical Instrument Series.

Several fictional works based on real people from the world of violin making were both entertaining and source material. William Alexander Silverman's *The Violin Hunter* is one; John Hersey's *Antonietta* is the other. And anyone interested in fiddles should try to see the movie *The Red Violin*. I've watched it half a dozen times and, while working on this book, told questioners many dozens of times that, no, I was not writing a book like *The Red Violin*.

If one were to be inspired to try making a violin at home, then Joseph V. Reid's *You Can Make a Stradivarius Violin* would be a decent place to start, though I can assure you that it's not as easy as he makes it seem.

Gene Drucker's recording of J. S. Bach's unaccompanied sonatas and partitas for violin has been reissued by Parnassas Records. I referred to enclosed liner notes written mostly by Drucker. I also used *The New Bach Reader: A Life of Johann Sebastian Bach in Letters and Documents*.

The recordings by the Emerson Quartet on Deutsche Grammophon are extensive, and all are worth listening to. Those I used most were *Mendelssohn: The Complete String Quartets* (2005), which includes a documentary video on the recording of the Octet; *Bach: The Art of the Fugue* (2003); *Beethoven: The Late Quartets*.

Glossary

THE MAIN PARTS OF A VIOLIN:

Back. The underside of the *sound box*, usually made of maple, sometimes one piece, but most often two pieces joined lengthways. The back is slightly arched, and the pattern of the wood is a main visual feature of the fiddle.

Bass-bar. A carefully carved rod of spruce that is glued to the inside of the violin *top*, on the bass side of the *bridge*.

Belly. (also Front or Top) The upper side of the *sound box*. It is almost always made of spruce in one, or two, joined pieces, arched and carefully graduated in thickness. Two *f-holes* are cut into it.

Block. Carved pieces of softwood—often spruce or willow—glued inside the *sound box* to support the *ribs* and hold them in place.

Bridge. An elaborately carved, thin piece of wood with two feet that rest on the belly and four small slots on top that hold the strings, whose tension keeps the bridge in place.

F-holes. Two holes cut into the violin belly on either side of the bridge in the shape of cursive Fs. They allow air carrying the violin's sound to escape from the *sound box.*

Fingerboard. A long piece of ebony that is attached to the *neck*, running most of the length of the strings. It supplies a surface against which the violinist's fingers can press the strings to change pitch.

Neck. A carved piece, usually maple, attached at its bottom to the violin *sound box* and at its top holding the *pegbox* for string tuning and the decorative *scroll.*

Pegbox. A small carved wooden box at the top of the neck, into which are inserted four pegs that hold one end of the strings and allow for tuning the instrument.

Purfling. A narrow inlaid band of three wood strips—the outer two dark and the inner light—that runs just inside the border edge of the belly and back. It is decorative but also serves to protect the edges and control cracks.

Ribs. Usually six strips of thin maple that form the curving sides of the *sound box*, connecting the belly and back.

Scroll. The ornamental carved piece at the top of the neck, traditionally done in a nautilus-like spiral.

Sound box. The resonant chamber formed by the belly, back, and ribs.

Sound post. A rod of wood, usually spruce, that is wedged into the *sound box*, under one foot of the bridge. Its function is to transfer vibration from the belly to the back, and its minute movement—called an adjustment—can significantly change the sound of the fiddle and its feel to the violinist.

About the author

About the book

Read on

Insights,
Interviews
& More . . .

Meet John Marchese

Marion Ettlinger

JOHN MARCHESE is a musician and award-winning journalist whose previous book is *Renovations: A Father and Son Rebuild a House and Rediscover Each Other*, published in 2001 by Riverhead. After studying music earlier in his education, he received a journalism degree from Temple University and became a staff writer for *Philadelphia* magazine, where he won a National Headliner Award for feature writing and shared a National Magazine Award. Since he moved to New York nearly twenty years ago, his work has appeared in dozens of publications, including the *New York Times*, *Esquire*, *GQ*, *Discover*, *Premiere*, *Rolling Stone*, *Worth*, *This Old House*, *Men's Journal*, and *Men's Health*. In more than twenty-five years as a trumpet player, he has performed with orchestras, big bands, jazz groups, and the Ringling Bros. and Barnum & Bailey circus.

A Conversation with John Marchese

You are an accomplished musician who still plays regularly. What drew you to music as a child? Why did you choose the trumpet?

I'm not quite sure what sparked my first interest in music. There weren't the usual influences. Nobody in my family played an instrument. There wasn't even much music played around the house. Until my sister became a teenager and got a little suitcase-sized record player, we didn't even own a stereo system. But when we finally got a turntable in the house, my uncle, who worked as a machinist in a record factory in our town, started bringing us stacks of free records—Sinatra, Nat King Cole, Broadway cast albums, and the Beatles for my sister.

I gravitated to Sinatra and Nat King Cole. Around the same time—I would have been around seven—the one television in the house ended up in my bedroom for some reason, and I got into the habit of watching late-night TV. I remember my second grade teacher's shock when I told the class that my favorite TV program was *The Tonight Show Starring Johnny Carson*. Of course, he always had a great jazz big band, and the leader, Doc Severinsen, made playing the trumpet seem really cool. So in seventh grade, when I had a chance to take up an instrument, I chose the trumpet. My talent was not particularly evident early on, but my interest was. I like to say that I was the only kid whose parents had to plead with him to *stop* practicing. ▶

> " I like to say that I was the only kid whose parents had to plead with him to *stop* practicing. "

A Conversation with John Marchese
(continued)

And why do you think you stayed with it when so many people give up playing a musical instrument as they get older?

Somehow—again, not because there was any evidence of strong talent—I started college as a music student, and after a couple of false starts, ended up trying to make a living through most of my twenties as a musician. I really did play everything from *Madame Butterfly* to the Ringling Bros. circus, and lots in between. But it was often very hard to actually pay the rent and buy food, so when the opportunity arose for me to work as a writer, I took it. Another thing I like to say is that I may be the only writer who got into it for the money. And, as Humphrey Bogart says in *Casablanca* about having come to North Africa for the waters, "I was misinformed."

I had pretty much given up music altogether when I was assigned to write a profile of Tony Bennett for the *New York Times* in 1994. He convinced me to take it up again, suggesting that I treat it as he does drawing and painting—as a strong avocation that sometimes people pay you to do. He was very sincere and inspiring, so I took some lessons to get back on track and have been playing—more or less—ever since. Music is the greatest hobby there is because it is intellectual, emotional, expressive, and also has a strong physical component that is often overlooked. If you work hard enough at it to become good, it's physically addictive—kind of like golf, but much less expensive.

Is there anything you learned about music from watching an instrument being made that you feel you couldn't have learned watching it being played?

Yes. It confirmed my long-held notion that music is much more of a blue-collar craft than many people imagine. Most of the musicians I've worked with over the years operate at the level of tradesmen. They're the folks you see backing up a singer on television, at a concert, recording jingles, or even playing at a wedding. They develop the skills to walk into a variety of musical situations and perform at a high level of craftsmanship. If sometimes they also cross that magical line into that realm that could be called art, terrific.

In my time with Sam Zygmuntowicz, he often talked about how making an instrument is—and should be—an honorable trade, something you practice with concentration and regularity with the aim that you'll achieve a level of skill such that your work on a bad day is still good. It's like being a plumber. In the book, Sam teasingly talks about people who are attracted to instrument making because it seems like an alternative lifestyle with a glamorous side. I came to feel that there was something special about Sam's workshop, but it was in the attitude he took and the spirit with which he approached his trade. There really wasn't anything glamorous about it. Watching Sam scrape and carve away at wood day after day made me realize anew that music is usually practiced in the same way. Whatever art there is comes as a by-product of the craft. ▶

> **Music is much more of a blue-collar craft than many people imagine.**

A Conversation with John Marchese
(continued)

What was your favorite part about watching Sam work on Eugene Drucker's violin? What was your least favorite part?

Favorite and least favorite were the same—Sam's talking so much. And that is not meant as any criticism of Sam. He is an interesting and thoughtful guy, and quite smart. And he has spent many, many years thinking about what he does. Obviously, I had to impose on him to explain what he was thinking while he was working. He was a very good sport about doing that. But, of course, a good deal of the time I got lost in the detail and nearly drowned in the depth, especially in the beginning. Luckily, I was taping during nearly all of our time together, which allowed me to go over his spoken thoughts a number of times to better understand them and put them into context.

Other than that, I would say the finish of the purfling was my least favorite thing. That rabbit-hide glue they use to stick the stuff on really smells funky.

When you set out to write the book, did you think you would discover the answer to why Stradivari's violins are so special? And were you disappointed to learn that there is no "secret" behind his instruments?

Well, I'm not completely sure even now that there isn't some kind of secret in Strad's work. But as the Italian violin maker Francesco Bissolotti told me on my trip to Cremona, the secret is being able to do it.

Rather than his using a secret varnish recipe or some kind of unique wood, I'm more inclined to believe that the Old Guy, as Sam so often called Stradivari, was just the best ever, working in a different time with different circumstances and different materials—none of which can be recreated. What I can't quite understand is why the violin world can't simply move on. At the risk of quoting Fitzgerald completely out of context, so many violinists are borne back ceaselessly into the past. Not only has that created a marketplace that supports those absurdly high prices for a relative handful of instruments, it feeds a kind of cult that, to me, seems ultimately unhealthy.

Of course, I've never cradled a Stradivari under my chin and heard what it would sound like under my ear.

Were you inspired to try to learn to play the violin?

Tempted a few times, but never inspired enough. Fortunately, I know how hard it is to play any instrument decently and realized it would be foolish to even try a new one. Sam told me that there is actually a school of thought that says that violin makers are better off not being able to play at all, because if they played the instruments they build, they would only get a distorted sense of the sound based on their own necessarily limited abilities. Besides, I didn't want to get one of those funny callouses on my neck.

I did at one point come close to trying ▶

> " At the risk of quoting Fitzgerald completely out of context, so many violinists are borne back ceaselessly into the past. "

A Conversation with John Marchese
(continued)

to build a violin. In my very first foray of research, when I was visiting the annual violin makers' conference in Oberlin, one of the makers handed me a big gouger and let me dig away at the back of a cello. It was fun, but I was scared to death I would punch a hole right through it and ruin the whole thing. At that stage the work was so preliminary, I couldn't have done any real damage. Still, I think it was probably a good decision to remain simply a fly on the wall when it came to violin making.

Did you discover anything interesting in your research that you had to leave out of the book?

Well, I didn't get into the whole mythology of the legendary Paganini, who I believe was the first violinist reputed to have sold his soul to the devil. And I didn't feel there was room to explore the recent bizarre case in which a group of old Italian fiddles were bestowed on the New Jersey Symphony Orchestra by a philanthropist and collector who later was accused of substantially inflating the value of the instruments. That seemed to be more about violin dealing than violin making. But it could—and should—be a whole other book.

The one great anecdote that I had hoped to squeeze into the book but could never find a place for was the old routine that Jack Benny used to do with his famous Stradivari violin. He would proudly display the fiddle for a guest, who would look inside at the label and say something like, "Boy, seventeen ten—if this violin is so good, why was it so cheap!?"

Benny would do his patented double take and say, "That's the *year*, not the price!" ⌒

The Violin Maker
An Update

DURING THE WEEKS when I was checking details and putting the final touches on the manuscript of this book, I was in contact with Sam Zygmuntowicz and Gene Drucker a number of times about the status of the Drucker fiddle in Gene's professional life. Sam was busy with other work, but being reminded that Drucker had not fallen in love with his new violin seemed to raise a challenge for the violin maker. The craftsman and musician had already been working together to alter the instrument so it would be more to Gene's liking. But still the violinist was not completely satisfied.

© Melissa Hamburg

The author with Sam Zygmuntowicz

So Sam harked back to the lessons he'd learned from his father, the laundryman: do whatever it takes to serve the customer. He offered Drucker a trade-in for another fiddle.

"I had another client who is not a professional, but who is very interested in fiddles," Sam told me. "He had brought back an instrument I made for him that was based on a Strad model—a 1732 Strad

> **Sam was busy with other work, but being reminded that Drucker had not fallen in love with his new violin seemed to raise a challenge for the violin maker.**

called the Busch." That instrument was made late in Stradivari's life, and oddly, some of the instruments of that period are quite similar to the Old Guy's work from when he was still a young guy. "There are many things in common between the Strad that Gene owns and this violin," Sam said. "When I built it, it wasn't intended to be an exact copy, but in effect it's more like Gene's Strad than the first instrument I built for him. Maybe I should have made something more like this one in the first place."

Drucker took the fiddle based on the Busch Strad home and almost from the start felt more comfortable playing it. "I agree with Sam that it's a much better match for me," Drucker told me. He used this new instrument for a series of Emerson String Quartet concerts at Carnegie Hall in the spring of 2007, and then continued to use it for a number of concerts as the Emerson toured through that year.

(In the meantime, Sam had built a fiddle for the superstar violin soloist Joshua Bell. One day, Bell was visiting Sam's studio and saw the newly available Drucker violin. He played it, liked the feel and sound, and took it home with him.)

Of course, although he felt better with his new violin, Drucker was still Drucker, always searching for that small thing that stood between him and perfection. The two men got together again to remake the bridge. Sometimes Gene would prefer to play the new violin, and sometimes he'd feel better on his original Stradivari.

"I'll never be able to give up the Strad," Gene decided, "but will probably alternate (and sometimes drive myself crazy) depending on the repertoire and acoustical space." ▶

> ❝ Of course, although he felt better with his new violin, Drucker was still Drucker, always searching for that small thing that stood between him and perfection. ❞

• • •

In the summer of 2007, Drucker's first novel, which he had worked on sporadically for thirty years, was published. Titled *The Savior*, it tells the story of a young German violinist who is forced to perform during World War II for prisoners at a concentration camp as part of a sadistic commandant's bizarre experiment. The reviews were overwhelmingly positive, and there was a surge of interest in the violinist and his book. One blistering-hot night in July, I joined Drucker at a bookstore near Lincoln Center and interviewed him about the book before a standing-room-only audience.

Before our talk, Drucker performed the Bach Chaconne for solo violin. I met him in a small greenroom before his performance and sat for a while in this tiny, airless closet while he warmed up on the 320-year-old fiddle called the Rosgonyl. Listening, I realized that as much as I might suspect that there was a bit of mass hypnosis at work in the cult of Stradivari, he made beautiful instruments that somehow made great players *feel* better. While it seemed to me that Gene Drucker could make music playing a shoebox with strings attached, hearing him play his Strad in these close quarters brought me back full circle to the early days of my research and the then novel notion of a "magical box."

"I'm not ready to believe that quality is merely a myth attached to the antique value of the old instruments," he would tell me later.

Sam Zygmuntowicz was leaning in the

66 It seemed to me that Gene Drucker could make music playing a shoebox with strings attached. 99

other direction. He continued to make new instruments—often for people who owned very valuable and famous old instruments. With clients like Drucker, Joshua Bell, Jimmy Lin, and Yo-Yo Ma, he was constantly in direct competition with the Old Guy. "Sam is a brilliant maker," Drucker wrote me once in an e-mail, "but for his instrument to beat out a Strad on every level is setting the bar very high."

For his part, Sam continued to feel he was getting closer to clearing that bar. "It used to be my assumption that you can't out-Strad Strad, so you don't try," he told me. "But I feel like it's not quite as unobtainable as I thought. I feel like I'm getting a handle on it. There are now a number of people who have Strads and also have a fiddle of mine, and we sometimes compare and adjust them in tandem. There's not as much difference as you might think. And it's certainly not some mystical difference. It's something one can define and address particular aspects of."

By this time, I'd known Sam for some years, and I had seen a subtle but significant evolution in his approach—one best characterized by something he told me: "What I'm trying to do now is more about being a maker of *sound* rather than the maker of an instrument."

Not long after this book was first released, I went to England on a magazine assignment. Naturally, because it involved foreign travel, my fiancée insisted on coming along.

Dixie and I arrived at Heathrow ▶

Airport in the early morning, bleary with fatigue. I had to get to a university in the Midlands, and after picking up a car, buying a map, and figuring out how to drive on the wrong side of the road, we were tooling up the M6 when we realized that we were going to be driving right past Oxford. "We have to go to that museum and see the Messiah," Dixie said. And so began a long, tough journey.

I'm talking mostly about the lack of parking spaces in the historic and leafy university town, and the propensity of streets to suddenly become bicycle paths or narrow to impassable (but awfully quaint) cobblestone alleys. It was late afternoon by the time we finally ditched our car near Jesus College and started asking everyone on the street directions for the Ashmolean museum. Finally stepping inside, we went right to the reception desk to ask where we could find the famous Stradivari violin.

"I'm afraid we're closing soon," a woman told us.

"We're only here to see this one thing," I promised.

"Go right up the stairs and to the left."

After all I'd read about the Old Guy's perfectly preserved fiddle, I expected the Messiah to be held in a high-tech chamber like something from a *Mission: Impossible* movie. But Dixie and I strolled into a vaulted gallery, and there it was—a fiddle in a glass case. Sitting nearby was an older, unarmed guard in a sweater vest, who, if he was guarding this famous instrument, seemed to be doing so in his sleep.

Dixie and I soon had our noses pressed up against the glass case, marveling at how

> ❝ 'We have to go to that museum and see the Messiah,' Dixie said. And so began a long, tough journey. ❞

well preserved this nearly 300-year-old instrument was, commenting on the dark varnish, and surveying the pointed, mitered joints of the purfling. Like so many things you've heard about and read about then finally get to see, the fiddle seemed somehow small.

Our talk roused the "guard," who unfolded himself from his chair, walked over to us, and began a friendly, impromptu lecture about the violin. I tried to let him know politely that I already knew quite a bit about the Messiah. Then Dixie asked, "Does anyone ever play it?"

"Oh, no, miss," he said, in an accent quite similar to that of the talking lizard on the auto insurance commercials. "That wouldn't be allowed. You see, now, what's the worst thing that could happen?"

He paused a moment and peered at us as if he was really expecting an answer, and Dixie and I later decided that one of us should have had the presence of mind to blurt out: "It could be struck by a meteor!"

"Someone could start playin' the thing," the guard said, "and right then have a heart attack, fall over on the violin, and crush it."

We stared bug-eyed into the glass case at the world's most famous violin, imagining this disaster. The guard seemed satisfied that he'd impressed us with his shocking scenario and returned to his chair. After a few more minutes of looking at the remarkably preserved and perpetually untouched fiddle, Dixie and I headed for the museum gift shop, where I bought a postcard of the Messiah and mailed it to Sam Zygmuntowicz. ❧

> ❝ 'Someone could start playin' the thing,' the guard said, 'and right then have a heart attack, fall over on the violin, and crush it.' ❞

The Web Detective

For a video clip of Sam Zygmuntowicz talking about his research into violin acoustics, visit msnbc.com or newsweek.com and search "Zygmuntowicz."

String Theory: New Approaches to Instrument Design
A good article explaining the research of Sam and other top violin makers working with scientists is at www.nytimes.com/2006/11/28/science/28acou.html?_r=1&oref=slogin

When Great Art Meets Great Evil
This article about Eugene Drucker's novel connects to a short video of the violinist playing and talking about Bach's Chaconne: www.nytimes.com/2007/07/29/arts/music/29oest.html?ref=books

Emerson String Quartet
At the official Emerson String Quartet Web site, there is all sorts of information about the musicians and their recordings. This link allows you to access a free download of the musicians discussing the great composers of the string quartet repertoire interspersed with the group's recordings of that music: www.emersonquartet.com/artist.php?view=news&nid=492

Second Fiddle to an Old Master
For some of my ideas about the cult of Stradivari and the astronomical prices of old violins, see: www.nytimes.com/2007/04/07/opinion/07marchese.html